THE SECOND COMING OF
BABYLON

THE
SECOND
COMING OF
BABYLON

MARK HITCHCOCK

Multnomah®Publishers *Sisters, Oregon*

THE SECOND COMING OF BABYLON
published by Multnomah Publishers, Inc.
© 2003 by Mark Hitchcock

International Standard Book Number: 1-59052-251-6

Cover design by The Office of Bill Chiaravalle
Cover image of globe by Photonica/Gary Atkinson
Image of flag by Image Source Photography

Unless otherwise indicated, Scripture quotations are from:
New American Standard Bible®
©1960, 1977, 1995 by the Lockman Foundation.
Used by permission.

Other Scripture quotations are from:
Holy Bible, New Living Translation (NLT) © 1996.
Used by permission of Tyndale House Publishers, Inc.

Multnomah is a trademark of Multnomah Publishers, Inc.,
and is registered in the U.S. Patent and Trademark Office.
The colophon is a trademark of Multnomah Publishers, Inc.

Printed in the United States of America

For information:
MULTNOMAH PUBLISHERS, INC.
POST OFFICE BOX 1720
SISTERS, OREGON 97759
03 04 05 06 07 08—10 9 8 7 6 5 4 3 2 1 0

———

To Scot Overbey,
a faithful friend, fellow shepherd,
and colaborer for Christ.

TABLE OF CONTENTS

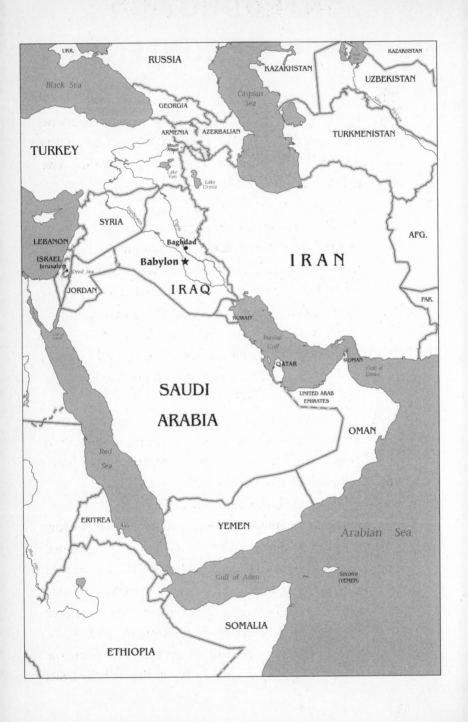

INTRODUCTION

On July 1, 2002, *TIME* magazine ran a cover article entitled "Apocalypse Now." The cover of the magazine read "The Bible & the Apocalypse: Why more Americans are reading and talking about the end of the world." The introduction to the article said:

> What do you watch for, when you are watching the news? Signs that interest rates may be climbing, maybe it's time to refinance. Signs of global warming, maybe forget that new SUV. Signs of new terrorist activity, maybe think twice about that flight to Chicago. Or signs that the world may be coming to an end, and the last battle between good and evil is about to unfold?[1]

Modern man is asking questions about the future as never before. People in every walk of life, from every background, wonder what tomorrow holds.

And they aren't all Bible students, either.

Although recent events have deepened the interest of many people in end-time Bible prophecy, they have also broadened and popularized this interest among others who had never paid much attention to such things before. For the Bible is the only place where man can find the answers, and everyone wants to know what the Bible says about how the world will end.

The nightly news is dominated by headlines from the Middle East. Homicide bombers in Israel. Reprisals by Israel into Palestinians towns. Iranian nuclear plants. North Korean missiles discovered on a ship headed for Yemen. Are the Saudis for us or against us?

And then of course, there's Iraq. Public enemy number one.

The terrorism alert system reminds us every day that we are in a long war against nameless murderers, bent on destroying our way of life. People everywhere are looking at the world much differently than they did just a few years ago. I know I do. We are wondering like never before if the world as we know it is clicking down to the last few seconds.

Consider these statistics. According to a *TIME/CNN* poll, since the attacks of September 11,

- 35 percent of Americans are paying more attention now to how the news might relate to the end of the world.

- 17 percent believe that the end of the world will happen in their lifetime.

- 59 percent believe that the prophecies of the *Book of Revelation* will come true.[2]

More than ever before, people are looking at world events through "prophetic eyes." This is probably true in your own life. Haven't you watched the news from a different perspective in the last year or so? How many times have you caught yourself wondering how the latest developments might relate to the end times?

In this small book we'll explore some of those developments together. We'll see how events in our world today, *especially in Iraq,* foreshadow what the Bible says about the end of the age.

But just to make sure we're all on the same page before we start, let's do a brief review and define five of the key terms you will see sprinkled throughout the pages of this book.

THE RAPTURE OF THE CHURCH TO HEAVEN

The Rapture is an event that, from the human perspective, can occur at any moment. There is nothing that *must* happen before the Rapture can take place. It's a signless event. When the Rapture occurs, all who have personally trusted in Jesus Christ as their Savior—the living and the dead—will be caught up to meet the Lord in the air. They will go with Him back up to heaven, then return with Him to earth at least seven years later at His second coming (see John 14:1–3; 1 Corinthians 15:50–58; 1 Thessalonians 4:13–18).

THE SEVEN-YEAR TRIBULATION PERIOD

The Tribulation is the final seven years of this age, which will begin with a peace treaty between Israel and Antichrist. It will end with the second coming of Christ back to earth. During this time the Lord will pour out His wrath upon the earth in successive waves of judgment. But the Lord will also pour out His grace by saving millions of people during this period (see Revelation 6–19).

THE THREE-AND-A-HALF-YEAR WORLD EMPIRE OF ANTICHRIST

During the last half of the Tribulation, Antichrist will rule the world politically, economically, and religiously. The entire world will give allegiance to him—or suffer persecution and death (see Revelation 13:1–18).

THE CAMPAIGN OF ARMAGEDDON

The Campaign or War of Armageddon is the final event of the Great Tribulation, when all the armies of the earth gather to come against Israel and attempt once and for all to eradicate the Jewish people (see Revelation 14:19–20; 16:12–16; 19:19–21).

THE SECOND COMING OF CHRIST TO EARTH

The climactic event of human history is the literal, physical, visible, glorious return of Jesus Christ back to planet earth to destroy the armies of the world gathered in Israel. He will then set up His kingdom on earth that will last for one thousand years (see Revelation 19:11–21).

God's Blueprint for the End Times

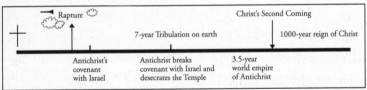

My prayer and heartfelt desire is that you will be a part of that kingdom. May God use this book in your life to help you trust His Word more fully, see His sovereign control more clearly, and live for Him more faithfully.

Maranatha!
—MARK HITCHCOCK

CHAPTER ONE

PROPHECY
IN THE
NEW MILLENNIUM

A few years ago I had the privilege of meeting a man who was 106 years old. It was quite an experience. He showed me his medals from World War I. He even had a certificate signed by President Woodrow Wilson.

We talked about many things, but the one question I most wanted to ask him was what he thought about all the changes in the world that had occurred during a lifetime that spanned the entire twentieth century. As I listened to his answers and thought about his life, I was struck by an astounding thought.

When this man was born, life was pretty much the way it had been for hundreds of years. People got around on foot, on horses, in wagons or carriages. Light and heat came from fireplaces, candles, and oil-fed lamps and lanterns. Bathrooms were outside. Communication was slow. Wars were fought with guns, knives, and crude artillery.

But suddenly that all changed.

Just think of all that man had witnessed in his lifetime! Inventions began to pop from laboratories, classrooms, and garage workshops with bewildering regularity. In a matter of one hundred years he saw electricity roll across America. He witnessed the advent of . . . telephones . . . television . . .

automobiles . . . planes . . . air conditioning . . . rockets . . .
missiles . . . a man on the moon . . . atomic weapons . . .
satellites . . . space-borne telescopes . . . unmanned space flights
to the far reaches of our solar system . . . fax machines . . .
VCRs . . . computers . . . DVDs . . . e-mail . . . cell phones . . .
laptop computers . . . and the Internet.

Who knows what will come next?

Who can even imagine?

Technology is exploding so quickly that none of us can
keep up with it.

And yet the torrid, ever accelerating pace of change
seems to be giving people a sense that something ominous is
on the horizon. We wonder how long weapons of mass
destruction can be kept out of the hands of madmen. How
long can tensions in the Middle East be held in check? *How
many small explosions does it take to ignite one that will shake
the whole world?*

To help us gain a little perspective, let's step back and take
a quick survey of the last fifty to sixty years. Perhaps it can
help us see where we may be headed in the new millennium.

FIFTY YEARS IN REVIEW

The last half of the twentieth century brought some
incredible changes, with ripple effects that rock the world
community to this day. None of the events in the last fifty
years are direct fulfillments of Bible prophecy, but they
bear amazing correspondence to the picture the Bible
paints of the end times. They show how world events
seem to be shaping up for the final Middle East conflict
presented in the Bible.

Here are nine of the most important events that have set the stage for the final showdown.

WORLD WAR II

Two twentieth-century wars provided the necessary impetus for the reuniting of Europe—the core of the historical Roman Empire. Of course, I'm referring to World War I and World War II. For centuries, the nations of Europe had fought one another again and again. But in the aftermath of World War II, a dramatic change occurred. Instead of building up for the next great armed conflict as they had done with depressing regularity for almost 1,600 years, they decided—almost inexplicably—to come together in a coalition of nations originally known as the Common Market.

Think about it! For the first time in 1,600 years the necessary preconditions for a reunited, revived Roman Empire, the second stage of the Roman Empire predicted by the prophet Daniel, were suddenly wrestled into place. Peaceful relations between the nations of Europe are a necessary prelude to the revival of the Roman Empire, as prophesied in the Bible.

The reunification began officially in 1957 with the Treaty of Rome. Since then, one by one, gradually yet steadily, the nations of Europe have come together. And this entire, revolutionary process has taken place in just forty-five years.

THE BOMB

The whole world changed on August 6, 1945, when the atom bomb fell on the Japanese city of Hiroshima. The most destructive weapon in human history had been loosed, containing more power than twenty thousand tons of TNT and producing more than two thousand times the blast of the most powerful bomb ever dropped up to that moment. A column of smoke billowed twenty thousand feet above Hiroshima.

In a recent ranking of the top one hundred news events of the last one hundred years, the dropping of the first atomic bomb was ranked number one. This singular event meant that any nation or rogue state that could attain this weapon would possess incredible power and leverage in dealing with other nations. The advent of the atomic age made it necessary for nations to make non-proliferation treaties, to work together to make sure these weapons did not fall into the wrong hands, to find ways to settle their differences peacefully. This is consistent with the picture of nations forging alliances in the end times.

THE HOMECOMING

God's Word predicts that, in the end times, the Jewish people will return to their ancient homeland and Israel will once again become a nation. Almost every prophecy of the end times is somehow related to the existence of Israel as a nation. Prophecy teachers had taught for years that Israel had to be regathered.

In the 1940s, who would ever have believed that the Jewish people would have a national homeland by 1948? The Jewish people were exiled from their homeland in A.D. 70. It had been almost 1,900 years! It was unthinkable. But the Jews endured the horror of the Nazi death camps, and within a few years thousands of them were home. Over the past fifty years, millions of Jews have returned to Israel. About 37 percent of the Jews in the world now live there.

The current and continuing stream of Jews back to Israel is setting the stage for Antichrist's peace covenant with Israel that will trigger the seven-year Tribulation (see Daniel 9:27).

THE RISE OF ISLAM (THE IRANIAN REVOLUTION)

Militant Islam has come out of nowhere in the last few years to become the greatest threat to world peace. The movement didn't really get started, however, until 1979, with the Iranian revolution under Ayatollah Khomeini. But revolution was quickly exported to other nations and today is our own nation's greatest concern.

The Bible predicts that a group of nations from all sides of Israel—all Islamic nations except Russia—will invade Israel in the end times (see Ezekiel 38–39).

What we have witnessed in the last two decades is another piece of the stage furniture being moved into place.

THE WALL CAME TUMBLIN' DOWN

I will never forget watching television on November 9, 1989, and not believing my eyes. The Berlin Wall was coming down. The twenty-seven-mile wall symbolized the Iron Curtain that separated East from West. Its fall signaled the defeat of Soviet communism and the liberation of Europe's captive nations.

The fall of communism and the liberation of Eastern Europe is in keeping with the biblical prediction of the unification of Europe in the end times. The fall of the Berlin

Wall, however, was only a harbinger of even greater trouble for the Soviet Empire.

THE END OF AN EMPIRE

When I was growing up the Soviet Union was the evil empire. We used to go through drills at school in case we were ever attacked by nuclear warheads. We all thought that, if this evil menace could be eliminated, the world would be safe. But in that era, the fall of the Soviet empire seemed like a fantasy. How could it ever happen apart from an apocalyptic World War III?

In fact, on September 17, 1955, in a speech in Moscow, Nikita Khrushchev made this famous statement about the invincibility of the Soviet Union: "If anyone believes that our smiles involve abandonment of the teaching of Marx, Engels, and Lenin, he deceives himself. Those who wait for that must wait until a shrimp learns to whistle."

On Thursday, December 21, 1991, the shrimp whistled.

The unthinkable occurred. The mighty Soviet Union as we had known it for seventy years simply faded away—not with a bang, but with a whimper. The dissolution that began with the fall of the Berlin Wall overwhelmed the entire USSR. The empire dissolved and fragmented into separate sovereign nations, corresponding to many of the republics that existed before the Soviets took over.

The fall of the Soviet Union had at least three significant stage-setting effects for the events of the end times.

1. First, the fall of the Soviet Union left Russia with a devastated economy and a humiliated national ego.

2. Second, the great Soviet collapse left a major power vacuum in Central Asia and the Middle East, which has since been filled by militant Islam. The modern rise of militant Islam began in 1979, as we have seen. But the movement gathered great impetus when the Soviet Union was no longer there as a check. In a way we might never have anticipated, the dissolution of the Soviet Union has made the world a much more dangerous place than it was before. When the Soviet Union existed the world knew only two superpowers, both in approximate balance, and both considered rational. Now the balance of power has been thrown into confusion. No longer does the balance-of-power equation recognize just two players—it's now a dozen or more.

    The world is more at risk for a global holocaust than at any time in history. Nuclear weapons can easily fall into the hands of irrational, fanatical leaders. North Korea is a perfect example. They will gladly sell nuclear weapons and technology to the highest bidder. And fomentation of anti-Western attitudes in the Islamic world could ignite into a jihad, or holy war.

    I believe that the ongoing deterioration of conditions in Russia, coupled with the rise of militant Islam, are paving the way for the Russian-Islamic invasion of Israel predicted

by the Jewish prophet Ezekiel more than
2,500 years ago (see Ezekiel 38–39).

3. Third, when the Soviet Union fell, it brought
    about a complete change in the alignment of
    nations in Europe. While this realignment
    does not fulfill a specific biblical prophecy, it
    lines up with the biblical prediction of a uni-
    fication of nations in the end times. The
    Bible predicts that a ten-kingdom form of
    the ancient Roman Empire will be reunited.
    Currently, eight nations from the former
    Soviet Union are slated to join the European
    Union (EU) on May 1, 2004.

The breakup of the Soviet Union has moved the EU a giant
step forward toward the reunification of the Roman Empire.

THE PERSIAN GULF WAR

The Gulf War caused quite a stir. For the first time in
modern history, armies from all over the world assembled
their troops in the Middle East. The troops gathered to liber-
ate Kuwait from Iraq and to stop any further aggression.
People everywhere, even in the secular media, wondered if
this military buildup was connected in some way to biblical
predictions about Armageddon. This war also provided the
first war broadcast live on CNN for the whole world to
watch (Vietnam wasn't the same—it wasn't shown in real
time). Every night we saw missiles and bombs hit their targets
with incredible precision. Saddam shot his Scud missiles
into Israel. And the world held its collective breath, wonder-

ing if Israel would unleash its military might against Iraq.

The Gulf War of the early 1990s didn't fulfill any specific biblical prophecies. But it did create a climate of prophetic expectation as the armies of the world—joined by the armies of the worldwide media—gathered in the Middle East.

It also brought attention to the nation of Iraq.

And Iraq is the home of ancient Babylon.

THE ONGOING MIDDLE EAST "PEACE PROCESS"

Ever since the Jewish people returned to their land in 1948, the Arab/Islamic nations that surround them have worked relentlessly to push them into the sea. Every Arab nation today—with the exception of Jordan and Egypt—is in a declared state of war with Israel right now.

The Israeli-Palestinian problem continues to fester like an infected boil. There is no end in sight. The horror of the homicide bombers has become so commonplace that it hardly even makes front-page news anymore. The world yearns for peace, especially in the Middle East.

The Bible says that Antichrist, who will rise from Europe, will come to power on a platform of peace. At first he will conceal his iron fist in a velvet glove. The act that catapults him onto the international scene is a seven-year peace treaty, or covenant, with Israel (see Daniel 9:27). The Antichrist emerges as the rider on a white horse, a false messiah, who conquers bloodlessly by means of diplomacy (see Revelation 6:1–2).

Then, after three and a half years, Antichrist takes off his mask and shows the world who he really is.

The city of Jerusalem continues to be the main sticking

point in the negotiations for peace. Jerusalem is at the center of all the controversy.

What we see on television every day looks strikingly similar to the biblical picture of the end times. The Bible predicts that in those days all eyes will once again be on Jerusalem. It will be the focus of the international community and an unsolvable dilemma.

Zechariah 12:2–3 says, "'Behold, I am going to make Jerusalem a cup that causes reeling to all the peoples around. . . . It will come about in that day that I will make Jerusalem a heavy stone for all the peoples; all who lift it will be severely injured. And all the nations of the earth will be gathered against it.'"

The current Middle East peace process and world focus on Jerusalem is another piece of the end-time puzzle that is falling into place.

THE AGE OF GLOBALIZATION

One final movement in the past century has helped pave the way for the end times . . . globalization. You can't hold it in your hand or watch it on television, because it's not quite as easily observed or defined as the other key events in the twentieth century. But it's just as real, and every bit as significant.

The 1990s were called the decade of globalization. Modern weapons, space technology, means of rapid travel, satellites, global surveillance, environmental issues, economic interdependence, and the prominent role of the United Nations have all worked together to create a particular environment in our contemporary world. We can now imagine how

PROPHECY IN THE NEW MILLENNIUM 23

one man—stepping into the right place at the right moment—could rule the whole world. Politically. Economically. Religiously. All of this is consistent with what we read in Revelation 13.

Until about twenty years ago, this was impossible. But given modern advances in technology, and man's recognition that cooperation is the only way to keep madmen in check, globalism is here to stay.

WHAT NEXT?

Stop and let this soak in. *All these events have happened in just a little more than fifty years.* Any single one, by itself, would be a significant signpost of end-time prophecy. But all of them together create an atmosphere of prophetic anticipation.

And that anticipation is growing by the hour.

As we take our first steps in the new millennium, we have to wonder what's next. When we juxtapose current developments alongside what has already transpired in the last few decades, those "signposts" turn into neon banners! Prophecy watchers expect the rapture of all believers in Christ to be the next great event.

Remember, no specific signs will precede the Rapture. It is a signless event that, as far as we know, could occur at any moment. It will occur before the beginning of the seven-year Tribulation period. At the end of the Tribulation, Jesus will return visibly, physically, and gloriously with His saints to slay the armies at Armageddon and establish His kingdom on earth.

The signs we see today are signs of the second coming of Christ back to earth to rule and reign, *not* specific signs of the Rapture. This is an important distinction. However, if we can already see signs of the Second Coming, the Rapture could be very soon.

As someone once said, "If you can see the signs of Christmas all around you and it's not even Thanksgiving yet, then you can expect that Thanksgiving is not far away."

Since the signs of the Second Coming are already casting their shadows into our day, it appears that the Rapture could be soon. If, however, God in His sovereign plan chooses not to rapture believers in the very near future, then what should we expect to see as the stage continues to be set for the end times? What should we expect in the new millennium? What developments should we continue to watch for?

Although I am neither a prophet nor the son of a prophet, I believe we can trace, from Scripture, some of the major trends we should expect.

Here are seven key prophetic indicators, or signs, that foreshadow what the Bible predicts for the end times.

1. Globalization will continue to accelerate, and the world will get smaller and smaller. It will also become a more dangerous place, forcing all of us to draw closer together and give up more and more personal freedom (see Revelation 13).
2. The EU will continue to expand and will centralize its power, making it easier for one man to come in and take control (see Daniel 7:8–28).
3. Radical Islam will continue to foment hatred for Israel and the West, with the total destruc-

tion of Israel as its main goal (see Ezekiel 38–39).

4. The Middle East peace process will continue to dominate world attention with no real, lasting solution in sight. The world will yearn for the man who can come and resolve this unsolvable problem (see Daniel 9:27).

5. Jerusalem will continue to be the major sticking point in the peace negotiations. No one will know what to do with the holy city (see Zechariah 12:1–3).

6. Oil will continue to draw the world eastward. The Middle East will be front and center. The rise in power of the Middle East is a significant event. From the standpoint of Bible prophecy this is one of the most dramatic signs that the world is shaping up for "closing time" (see Daniel 11:40–45).

7. Iraq will remain in the news as a major player in world politics. Iraq did not even become a modern nation until 1932. Although Iraq is an Arab nation, the Iraqis are really Babylonians. They trace their tribal, ethnic, cultural, and political heritage back to ancient Babylon. They are a proud people with a glorious history. So, as we look to the future it might *appear* that we are looking more and more to the past.

The ancient city of Babylon in modern Iraq will be rebuilt as a great commercial center (see Revelation 17–18).

The Bible never specifically calls this city "New" Babylon, but I believe this title is a perfect description of the city. Just as we name places "New" York, "New" Hampshire, and "New" Jersey, the rebuilt Babylon will emerge as a "new" city. Literally, we will see the "second coming of Babylon" for the end times.

Although the focus of this book is the New Babylon that will be built in Iraq, all these signs of the times are related. Bible prophecy is a matrix of interrelated events. When we talk about New Babylon, we'll find ourselves highlighting other major events of the end times as well.

PREPARING FOR THE END TIMES

The predicted events of the end times will not occur in a vacuum. Advance preparations must occur. I believe that the preparatory events and movements we are seeing now serve as discernible signs of the times. Current events in Iraq and the Middle East are preparing the world for the rebuilding of Babylon, as predicted in the Bible.

However, before we get into the specific Bible prophecies concerning Babylon in the end times, join me first in another quick glance at the bigger picture.

CHAPTER TWO

SENSATIONALISM
OR
SIGNS OF THE TIMES?

Anyone who writes a book that links "signs of the times" to current events will hear from critics who will refer to his work as "newspaper exegesis." Such critics will say that prophecy writers are making the Bible fit into current events rather than fitting current events into valid biblical interpretation.

I agree that there are some irresponsible end-time prophecy teachers and writers who do engage in newspaper exegesis. They try to make every current event fit somehow into the scheme of Bible prophecy. Every famine, earthquake, disease, war, and natural disaster is heralded as a sign that Jesus is coming soon. And often their interpretations seem to change with the headlines.

I know that some will make this same charge against me, that my views on the end times—especially the rebuilding of Babylon in modern Iraq—are based on Iraq's current prominence in the headlines. Some will say that I'm putting the cart before the horse, that I'm simply looking for Scriptures that can be twisted enough to correspond to what we see on the nightly news.

Let me head this charge off at the pass by pointing out that many respected Bible teachers wrote about Israel's regathering as a nation more than one hundred years before it occurred—when the very idea seemed preposterous. And at a time when it would have been humanly impossible for one man to gain control over our globe, others foresaw the emergence of Antichrist, the man who would rule the whole world.

The same dynamic is also true about the rebuilding of Babylon. The idea of the New Babylon is nothing new. It's been around for a long time. Many well-respected Bible teachers held and taught this view before Iraq became an independent nation in 1932—even before huge oil fields were discovered there, near Kirkuk, in 1927.

Of course, the fact that others in the past have agreed with my view does not, by itself, prove that my interpretation is correct. But it does show that respected scholars from different vantage points, working entirely on their own, have come to the same conclusion independently of one another.

VOICES FROM THE PAST

Here is just a small sampling of writers in the past who taught about a literal, rebuilt city of Babylon in the end times, long before the rest of us had ever heard of Saddam Hussein or the Gulf War crisis.

JOSEPH AUGUSTUS SEISS

J. A. Seiss was a Lutheran pastor and scholar who was born in 1823. Commenting on the identity of Babylon in Revelation 17, he said:

The realization is yet in the future, and we cannot speak with confidence as to how matters will eventuate; but there seems to be reason for the belief that the literal Babylon will be restored, and that we are to look to the coming up again of that primal city for the fulfillment of what is here foreshown.[3]

GEORGE HAWKINS PEMBER

G. H. Pember, writing in 1888, stated his belief that Babylon would be rebuilt—even though there was no evidence at the time that this could possibly occur.

...every principle of sound interpretation bids us to understand the eighteenth chapter as predicting the overthrow of a literal Babylon on the Euphrates, just before the appearing of the Lord Jesus in glory....The centre of God's action will then be removed from the West to the East, and be found once more in Jerusalem. Therefore, also, Satan will find it necessary to shift his base of operations from Western Rome to the East, and will again have need of his old stronghold, the city of the Euphrates....It seems, therefore, on every account likely that we may presently hear of projects to restore Babylon; and it is universally admitted by those who know the country, that its fertility and resources would prove as great as ever, if only a little pains were taken to develop them.[4]

CLARENCE LARKIN

Writing in 1919, Reverend Clarence Larkin believed in a literal rebuilt city of Babylon in the end times. He said, "That the ancient city of Babylon restored is to play an important part in the startling events of the last days of this Dispensation, is very clear."[5]

ARTHUR W. PINK

In his excellent 1923 summary of the biblical teaching on the Antichrist, A. W. Pink supported the view of a rebuilt Babylon in the end times.

> That there will yet be another Babylon, a Babylon eclipsing the power and glory of that of Nebuchadnezzar's day, has long been the firm conviction of the writer. Nor are we by any means alone in this conviction. A long list of honored names might be given of those who have arrived, independently, at the same conclusion that the Scriptures plainly teach that Babylon is going to be rebuilt. . . . The Word of God expressly affirms that Babylon will play a prominent part at the Time of the End.[6]

F. E. MARSH

In 1925, Bible teacher F. E. Marsh wrote an article entitled "Will Babylon be Rebuilt?" In the article he observed, "This writer believes Babylon—an actual city—will be rebuilt. We now give reasons why we believe there will be a rebuilt Babylon."[7]

WILLIAM R. NEWELL

In 1935, in his classic commentary on Revelation, Newell stated his belief in a rebuilt city of Babylon on the Euphrates in the end times, a city that would function as Antichrist's world commercial capital.

> We are forced then, to the conclusion, that the overthrow of Babylon, as the revealed center of iniquitous luxury and Satan-worship, the culmination of man's glory, lies yet in the future, in the land of Shinar, where Babylon's history began! . . . The final form of Babylon is the literal city on the Euphrates, rebuilt as Antichrist's capital of the last days, opposing Israel as God's earthly people who will have been gathered back to their land.[8]

None of these men could possibly have dreamed that Iraq, the land of ancient Babylon, would move to the center of the world stage as it has today. Yet they believed what they saw in the Scriptures. And amazingly, what these men saw in the Word of God, and accepted by faith, we are now witnessing with our own eyes. These men didn't develop their views on Babylon by looking at the headlines. There weren't any such headlines when they wrote! But what they believed is beginning to take shape. We see the signs all around us.

This should cause us to stop and think. Could the current events in the Middle East be setting the stage for the rebuilding of Babylon and the other key events that are part of the end-time drama?

FOCUSING ON THE FIG TREE

Jesus gave His disciples and us a general blueprint of what we should look for in the days just before His glorious return to earth.

The setting was Jesus' farewell message to his bewildered band of disciples. Jesus had been with them for more than three years—and they couldn't begin to comprehend what was about to happen to their leader. Two days later, on Friday, He would be nailed to a Roman cross and would suffer a cruel, barbaric death. But it was still Wednesday of the final week of His life, and from a hill east of Jerusalem called the Mount of Olives, Jesus was about to unveil a sweeping panorama of the future for His disciples.

Jesus and the Twelve slowly ascended the summit of the hill that overlooked the Temple Mount in Jerusalem two hundred feet below. It was Passover season, so the temple precinct would have been teeming with pilgrims. When they reached the summit, Jesus seated Himself on a rock, and four of the disciples—Peter, James, John, and Andrew—approached Him privately and asked a penetrating question that had probably been burning in their hearts for some time. "Tell us, when will these things happen, and what will be the sign of Your coming, and of the end of the age?" (Matthew 24:3).

The question they asked is one that many are asking today. "Rabbi, when will the world come to an end?" But notice that when Jesus' disciples asked Him, He didn't say, "Don't worry about signs of the end of the age." And He didn't say, "I'm not going to tell you; it's none of your business!" No; in Matthew 24:4–31 He outlined several general and specific signs of the end of the age.

After listing some of the main signs, Jesus concluded with the parable of the fig tree in Matthew 24:32–33. "Now learn a lesson from the fig tree. When its buds become tender and its leaves begin to sprout, you know without being told that summer is near. Just so, when you see the events I've described beginning to happen, you can know his return is very near, right at the door" (NLT).

Many believe that the picture of the fig tree is a reference to the nation of Israel, since the fig tree often represented Israel in the Old Testament. It seems more likely to me, however, that Jesus was simply using a natural illustration that anyone could understand. He was saying that, just as one can tell summer is near by the blossoming of the fig tree, so one can know when the end times are near by the signs of the times.

Of course, this doesn't mean that we can know the *exact* time of Jesus' coming. Date setting is strictly forbidden by Jesus. Date setters are always wrong. In order that no one will ever be mistaken on this subject, Jesus makes it absolutely clear just a few verses later, after His illustration of the fig tree.

In Matthew 24, Jesus warns, "But of that day and hour

no one knows, not even the angels of heaven, nor the Son, but the Father alone…. Therefore be on the alert, for you do not know which day your Lord is coming…. For this reason you also must be ready; for the Son of Man is coming at an hour when you do not think He will" (vv. 36, 42, 44).

Jesus strikes a perfect balance. We can never know the exact time of His coming. We must recognize that the Bible does not give us every detail about the end times, nor does it answer every possible question. But Jesus does say that we can discern signs that indicate the general season. Signs that His coming could be very near.

In other words, when the key places, players, and events are aligned consistent with the scenario depicted in God's Word, we are to pay attention and know that He could be coming soon.

BABYLON: A SIGN OF THE TIMES

Many today, even those who don't know a great deal about Bible prophecy, are becoming increasingly aware of the amazing correspondence between the clear trend of world events and what the Bible predicted thousands of years ago. The present alignment of several key prophetic signposts should grab our attention.

One of the places mentioned in Bible prophecy that seems to be lining up for the end times is Iraq, home of the ancient city of Babylon.

As we get a running start in the new millennium, one of the main issues in the world is what to do with Iraq. Why is Iraq dominating the news? Is it all just a coincidence?

BACK TO BABYLON

According to eyewitness reports, Saddam Hussein views himself as a new Nebuchadnezzar, as the leader of the new Babylonian empire that he has expected to expand into a pan-Arab alliance of nations. Saddam Hussein has already begun rebuilding the city of Babylon. His removal will result in the termination of the United Nations (UN) sanctions, and when the oil begins to flow freely again, efforts to rebuild the city can be redoubled as a link with Iraq's past glory, even though Saddam might no longer be in the picture.

Then the city will rise like the phoenix to take its appointed place on the end-time stage as one of the key places, just as the Bible predicts.

But before we get too far ahead of ourselves, let's take a look at what the Bible says about Babylon's notorious beginnings, in the book of Genesis.

CHAPTER THREE

FROM THE CRADLE TO THE GRAVE

I first heard the phrase "cradle of civilization" in my seventh-grade social studies class. Our teacher explained how the Tigris-Euphrates River valley was where it all began for the human race. All the great early civilizations were there: the Sumerians, the Assyrians, and the Babylonians. The word *Mesopotamia* literally means "the land between the rivers." Man got his start between the Tigris and Euphrates Rivers.

A few years later it struck me that the Bible says the very same thing. The book of beginnings, Genesis, teaches us that human history began in the river valley of the Tigris and Euphrates. Amazingly, the Bible also says that man's history in this age will end there as well.

Man's history—from the cradle to the grave—is tied to this river valley in general . . . and to Babylon in particular.

Let's trace what the Bible says. I think you'll be amazed at what we see. History is coming full circle. *The focus of world events is cycling back to where it all began.* I don't believe it's an accident. This is the exact scenario depicted in the pages of the Bible.

A RIVER RUNS THROUGH IT

When God created Adam from the dust of the ground and breathed life into his nostrils, the Bible says that God placed Adam in the Garden of Eden. "The LORD God planted a garden toward the east, in Eden; and there he placed the man whom He had formed" (Genesis 2:8).

One of the fascinating features of the garden God created is that it was watered by a river, which divided into four other tributaries.

> Now a river flowed out of Eden to water the garden; and from there it divided and became four rivers. The name of the first is Pishon; it flows around the whole land of Havilah, where there is gold . . . . The name of the second river river is Gihon; it flows around the whole land of Cush. The name of the third river is Tigris; it flows east of Assyria. And the fourth river is the Euphrates. Then the LORD God took the man and put him into the garden of Eden to cultivate it and keep it. (Genesis 2:10–11, 13–15)

Did you notice that two of the divisions of the Eden river are the Tigris and Euphrates rivers? The Bible clearly places man's beginning in Mesopotamia, the land between the rivers.

Of course, the paradise of the Garden was destroyed by the Flood in response to the unabated wickedness of man. But after this event man again returned to the Tigris-Euphrates valley.

Man went back to Babel.

And he will do it yet again.

A CITY AND A TOWER

After the worldwide flood, as the planet became repopu-
lated, the human race gathered itself into one place.
According to Genesis 10–11, Nimrod was the first leader of
the global community. The Bible says that Nimrod "became
a mighty one on the earth. He was a mighty hunter before
the LORD.... The beginning of his kingdom was Babel"
(Genesis 10:8–10).

The ancient Hebrew Scriptures also indicate that
Nimrod's nature was that of a tyrant, or dictator. You might
say he was the first world dictator, and his capital city was
Babylon. In this sense, Nimrod prefigures the final great
world ruler, the Antichrist, who will also locate his world
commercial capital at Babylon.

The method Nimrod and his followers—the first global-
ists—used to express their insolence toward God was the
building of a city and a tower. They shook their collective
fist in God's face and defied His command to scatter over
the face of the earth (see Genesis 9:1). They settled down in
the land of Shinar at Babel with a three-part plan:

1. to build a city,
2. to build a tower reaching to the heavens,
3. to make a name for themselves (to glorify man).

Genesis 11:1–9 makes all this very clear:

> *Now the whole earth used the same language
> and the same words. It came about as they
> journeyed east, that they found a plain in the
> land of Shinar and settled there. They said to
> one another, "Come, let us make bricks and*

burn them thoroughly." And they used brick for stone, and they used tar for mortar. They said, "Come, let us build for ourselves a city, and a tower whose top will reach into heaven, and let us make for ourselves a name, otherwise we will be scattered abroad over the face of the whole earth." The LORD came down to see the city and the tower which the sons of men had built. The LORD said, "Behold, they are one people, and they all have the same language. And this is what they began to do, and now nothing which they purpose to do will be impossible for them. Come, let Us go down and there confuse their language, so that they will not understand one another's speech." So the Lord scattered them abroad from there over the face of the whole earth; and they stopped building the city. Therefore its name was called Babel, because there the LORD confused the language of the whole earth; and from there the LORD scattered them abroad over the face of the whole earth.

The city and the tower represent the two aspects of Babylon that continue today: political power balanced against religious rebellion and apostasy.

The city they built represents the political unity of the city of Babylon. Babylon was a literal place ruled over by a literal king who exercised political power over all the inhabitants of the world. Note, also, the use of tar as mortar—those huge oil deposits, perhaps close enough to the surface to create tar pits, were useful even in ancient times!

Babylon also represents false religion. The first organized false religion has passed down from Babylon into all the other false religions of the world. Their tower symbolizes the religious unity that dominated Babylon. This *ziggurat,* intended by them to reach to the heavens, was no doubt intended to be a place of occult worship of the stars and heavens. Therefore, the first federation of man, the first "United Nations," was a society built to bring the human race together to exalt man and exclude God—to deify man and dethrone God.

John Walvoord provides an excellent summary of the Babylonian religious system.

> Babylon was important not only politically but also religiously. Nimrod, who founded Babylon (Gen. 10:8–12), had a wife known as Semiramis who founded the secret religious rites of the Babylonian mysteries, according to accounts outside the Bible. Semiramis has a son with an alleged miraculous conception who was given the name Tammuz and in effect was a false fulfillment of the promise of the seed of the woman given to Eve (Gen. 3:15).
>
> Various religious practices were observed in connection with the false Babylonian religion, including recognition of the mother and child as God and of creating an order of virgins who became religious prostitutes. Tammuz, according to the tradition, was killed by a wild animal and restored to life, a satanic anticipation and counterfeit of Christ's resurrection. Scripture condemns this false

> religion repeatedly (Jer. 7:18; 44:17–19, 25;
> Ezek. 8:14). The worship of Baal is related
> to the worship of Tammuz.... Babylon then
> is the symbol of apostasy and blasphemous
> substitution of idol-worship for the worship
> of God in Christ.[9]

The legend of Semiramis and Tammuz spread around the world. Their names were changed in different places, but the basic story remained the same. In Assyria, the mother was Ishtar, the son was Tammuz. In Phoenicia, the mother was Astarte and the son was Baal. In Egypt, she was Isis and her son was Osiris, or Horus. In Greece, she was Aphrodite and her son was Eros. For the Romans, the mother was Venus and the son was Cupid.

From the beginning, then, Babylon was both a town and a tower, a city and a system, a place and a philosophy. We will encounter this same twofold depiction of Babylon later when we look at Babylon in Revelation 17–18.

SATAN'S MASTER PLAN

The situation at Babylon in Genesis 10–11 played right into Satan's plan. While he is not mentioned by name, we can be certain that the old serpent introduced in Genesis 3 was working feverishly to energize this rebellious plan. In this setting he could influence and direct world affairs through one man. He controlled both the city (government) and the system (religion).

He could be "god" in the eyes of all men, through occult worship and practices. After all, this is his ultimate desire. At the same time, evil could spread through the whole race with ease, since everyone was in one place speaking one language. The masses could also be converted to his false religion, with little to stand in his way.

Of course, God was in total control. He saw what puny man was doing, and He came down and confounded man's language, scattering man all over the face of the earth (see Genesis 11:5–8). That was the official end of the first global community.

Globalism was put on hold.

But Satan wasn't finished.

He set out immediately to bring the world back together so he could control all of it once again. He set out to bring mankind back to Babylon where he could again control the whole world through one man.

In a sense, human history is the story of Satan working to bring man back to Babylon under his rule. This will finally happen according to Revelation 17–18. Both the city of Babylon and the false religious system of Babylon will be resurrected in the end times.

BACK EAST

As we can see from Genesis, man got his start in the East. The Bible says that man was placed in "a garden toward the east, in Eden" (Genesis 2:8). For the early millennia of man's history, the focus remained in the East. The great empires were all located there. But slowly that began to change. Since the fall of the Persian empire to Alexander the Great in 331 B.C., the main power centers of the world have slowly relocated to the West.

The four empires pictured in Daniel 2 reveal this westward drift. Babylon—Medo-Persia—Greece—Rome. Greece is west of Babylon and Persia. Rome is west of Greece. With the rise of the Roman empire, world power shifted dramatically to Europe. In later centuries, power continued to move west, to the British Empire and then on to the United States. And since then, for the most part, power has been concentrated in the West for two thousand years, especially in the last two hundred years.

But in the most recent decades, something incredible has begun to happen. Power and world attention has begun to return to the East. With little warning the East has risen again as a major player. Why? One word: *oil*.

This fact was brought to our attention in a dramatic way in 1973. At the end of the Six-Day War in 1967, it became apparent to Arab nations that they were no match, militarily, for Israel. And even if they could have cobbled together the military might to defeat Israel, they knew that they would still have to face the armed might of the United States, Israel's staunch ally.

As a result, a new strategy began to take shape in Arab capitals.

That new direction took on even greater urgency in the aftermath of the 1973 Yom Kippur War with Israel. The Arab alliance had been totally defeated and it became all too clear that a new kind of unity was essential. If they were ever to achieve the power they desired, it would have to be based on their trump card: control of the major oil reserves of the world.

As a result, in November, 1973, the Arab nations reduced their production of oil and instituted an embargo against nations that favored Israel—mainly the United States and the Netherlands. I still remember the long lines at gas stations, strong talk of gas rationing, nationwide reduction of the speed limit to fifty-five mph, and the fear of many that we would be crippled by insufficient fuel for heating homes, running our automobiles, and powering our military machine.

For the first time in centuries, the world looked east. At that point, the Middle East stepped back onto the world stage as a key player on the international scene. From that time on, oil prices and production figures have relentlessly drawn world attention to the East.

This is precisely what we should expect if the coming of Christ is near. The Bible says that the Middle East is the stage for the key events of the end times.

The East is back. And it is here to stay.

THE TALE OF TWO CITIES

From the very beginning, Babylon has been presented as man's city. Man built it to make a name for himself. But to an even greater extent it was also Satan's city. He was the power behind almost everything that went on there. Babylon was the first city built after the flood. It was the place man first gathered in collective rebellion against God. Indeed, *Babylon* literally means "city of confusion."

After chapters 10 and 11 of Genesis, Babylon is next mentioned in Genesis 14, when Chedorlaomer, the king of Elam, leads an invading force of four armies into the land of Canaan. Amraphel, the king of Shinar (Babylon), is not the official leader of this group, but for some reason he and his city get top billing. This is the first war recorded in the Bible, and Babylon is mentioned first! Once again, God seems to be focusing on Babylon to highlight its importance, even though it might not have been the main city in this particular story.

In contrast to Babylon, Jerusalem is pictured as God's city. Jerusalem is also mentioned for the first time in Genesis 14. Called Salem at that time, it's the city in which the mysterious figure named Melchizedek lived. After Abraham defeated Chedorlaomer, Melchizedek came out from Salem to meet him as he returned, bringing bread and wine. Interestingly, Melchizedek was "a priest of God Most High"; his name means "king of righteousness." *Salem* means "city of peace." Melchizedek was a king-priest of Salem/Jerusalem who prefigured the ultimate king-priest of Jerusalem, Jesus Christ (see Psalm 110:4–7; Hebrews 7:1–28).

About one thousand years later, God chose Jerusalem for King David to establish as his capital city. And later, under Solomon, it became the place in which God chose to come and dwell on earth in the Holy of Holies in the temple. In a very literal sense, Jerusalem is God's city on earth.

Although Jerusalem and Babylon first appear together in Genesis 14, the last time they appear together in the same book is in Revelation 17–18 (for Babylon) and Revelation 21:1–22:5 (for the New Jerusalem). Henry Morris, in his excellent commentary on Revelation, says, "The harlot Babylon is a contrasting type of the chaste Jerusalem and, in one sense, the whole course of history is essentially a tale of these two great spiritual cities."[10]

Compare what the Bible tells us about Jerusalem, God's own city, to what it tells us about Babylon:

Jerusalem-Babylon Comparisons	
Jerusalem	**Babylon**
Most mentioned city in the Bible	Second most mentioned city
City of peace	City of confusion and war
God's temple was there	Man's tower was there
River of God (see Revelation 22:1)	River Euphrates
Chaste bride, as described in Revelation 21:9–10: "'I will show you the bride, the wife of the Lamb.'. . . and [he] showed me the holy city, Jerusalem, coming down out of the heaven from God."	Great harlot, as described in Revelation 17:1, 3: "And he carried me away in the Spirit into a wilderness; and I saw a woman sitting on a scarlet beast, full of blasphemous names, having seven heads and ten horns."
Eternal, from God (see Revelation 21:2)	Destroyed by God (see Revelation 18:8)
God's city (see Revelation 21:2)	Satan's city (see Revelation 18:2)

The Bible ends as it begins—with man gathered in rebellion against God in Babylon (see Revelation 17–18). But all who humbly submit to God by putting their trust in Him have their part in the New Jerusalem, the city of eternal peace and rest.

FAST FORWARD

Babylon is the cradle of civilization. Man started his rebellion against God there, and it will end there when God comes to destroy the city once and for all. Babylon will rise again, but the result will be the same. Babylon will fall again. Only this time, Babylon will fall never to rise again.

Babylon the cradle will then become the grave.

CHAPTER FOUR

THE HEAD OF GOLD

There's an old Chinese proverb that says, "It's difficult to prophesy, especially about the future." We know this all too well. No man knows what will happen tomorrow, tonight, or even today, let alone next year.

God's Word is absolutely clear that only God knows the future (see Isaiah 41:21–23; 44:6–7). In fact, this is one of the major proofs that the Bible is the Word of God. It foretells future events with 100 percent accuracy, 100 percent of the time.

One of the great prophecies in the Bible is found in Daniel 2. It's often called the ABCs of Bible prophecy. In this chapter, the Jewish prophet Daniel was given a revelation by God that revealed not the next day or the next one hundred days, but what now has been more than 2,500 years. Of course, Daniel was not given every detail. But he was shown the major flow of world history from his own day in about 550 B.C. until the second coming of Jesus Christ to earth, to rule and reign forever. His incredible prophecy is as relevant today as it was the day it was written.

I HAD A DREAM

Daniel 2 opens in the year 602 B.C., in Babylon. At that time, the great Babylonian monarch, Nebuchadnezzar, was probably in his late twenties. He was the ruler of the world.

But he was restless. As the old saying goes, "Uneasy lies the head that wears the crown."

Nebuchadnezzar's uneasiness might have been one of the reasons why his forces undertook several military expeditions from 604–602 B.C. Egypt still remained a formidable opponent and was not finally subjugated until 570 B.C.

One night in 602 B.C., young Nebuchadnezzar was lying in bed thinking about his future and the future of his empire (see Daniel 2:29). He had seen other nations destroyed, even by his own hand. He had probably witnessed the fall of Nineveh just a few years earlier, in 612 B.C.

During the night, God responded to Nebuchadnezzar's desire by revealing the future to him in a dream that greatly troubled and perplexed him. When he awoke, Nebuchadnezzar knew that this dream was significant. He was so anxious to know its meaning that he called in all his counselors and advisers very early in the morning. He demanded that they do two things: (1) give him the content of his dream and (2) interpret its meaning. Daniel's account of the dream and its aftermath is fascinating.

> Now in the second year of the reign of Nebuchadnezzar, Nebuchadnezzar had dreams; and his spirit was troubled and his sleep left him. Then the king gave orders to call in the magicians, the conjurers, the sorcerers and the Chaldeans to tell the king his dreams. So they came in and stood before the king. The king said to them, "I had a dream and my spirit is anxious to understand the dream."
>
> Then the Chaldeans spoke to the king in

Aramaic: "O king, live forever! Tell the dream to your servants, and we will declare the interpretation." The king replied to the Chaldeans, "The command from me is firm: if you do not make known to me the dream and its interpretation, you will be torn limb from limb and your houses will be made a rubbish heap. But if you declare the dream and its interpretation, you will receive from me gifts and a reward and great honor; therefore declare to me the dream and its interpretation."

They answered a second time and said, "Let the king tell the dream to his servants, and we will declare the interpretation."

The king replied, "I know for certain that you are bargaining for time, inasmuch as you have seen that the command from me is firm, that if you do not make the dream known to me, there is only one decree for you. For you have agreed together to speak lying and corrupt words before me until the situation is changed; therefore tell me the dream, that I may know that you can declare to me its interpretation."

The Chaldeans answered the king and said, "There is not a man on earth who could declare the matter for the king, inasmuch as no great king or ruler has ever asked anything like this of any magician, conjurer or Chaldean. Moreover, the thing which the king demands is difficult, and there is no one else who could declare it to the king except gods, whose dwelling place is not with mortal flesh."

> *Because of this the king became indignant*
> *and very furious and gave orders to destroy all*
> *the wise men of Babylon. So the decree went*
> *forth that the wise men should be slain; and*
> *they looked for Daniel and his friends to kill*
> *them.* (Daniel 2:1–13)

The wise men of Babylon were not especially wise—but they knew enough to argue that no man could do what the king asked. No king had ever asked such a thing before! Filled with fear, they reluctantly confessed total inability to meet the king's demand.

Many people believe that Nebuchadnezzar had forgotten the dream and wanted his advisers to give him the dream for that reason. I don't think so! I believe he remembered the dream vividly. He asked his advisers to give him the dream and its interpretation knowing that, if they could give him the dream, their interpretation would be trustworthy. Anyone can offer an "interpretation" of a dream. But telling someone the content, too, is humanly impossible. If you can do the impossible, your interpretation must be true.

In his anger, Nebuchadnezzar issued the "Dunghill Decree." If they could not give him the dream and the interpretation, they would be torn limb from limb, and their homes would be reduced to rubbish, or dung heaps.

This certainly grabbed their undivided attention.

DANIEL AND THE DREAM

Since Daniel and his three Hebrew friends were part of Nebuchadnezzar's inner circle of counselors, they were covered by this edict as well. So Daniel interceded with Arioch, the king's bodyguard, for a brief stay of the execution. As a result of this conversation, Daniel actually went in before Nebuchadnezzar to ask for more time (see Daniel 2:14–16). Nebuchadnezzar was in no mood for delaying tactics, but there must have been something in this young Hebrew man that captivated the king. There was some kind of calm assurance that led the king to give a brief reprieve.

Knowing that time was short, Daniel called his friends together for a prayer meeting to ask God to give them the information they needed to stay alive (see Daniel 2:17–18). That night, in a vision, God revealed to Daniel both the dream and its interpretation.

Now, the natural response would be to rush in immediately before the king to give him the good news. But before going in, Daniel paused to bless the God of Heaven—to give God the glory for giving him the revelation (see Daniel 2:19–23).

The next morning, Daniel was led in before Nebuchadnezzar. In your mind you can just picture the scene. Nebuchadnezzar was seated on his throne—afraid, frustrated, and angry. He had no expectation that Daniel could do what none of his other charlatans were able to do.

Daniel first began by openly giving God all the credit for the revelation he had received and was about to reveal. He made it clear that he was just a channel used by the God of Heaven. Daniel then proceeded to tell Nebuchadnezzar what he was thinking about before he went to sleep the night he had the dream. "As for you, O king, while on your bed your thoughts turned to what would take place in the future" (Daniel 2:29).

At this point you can imagine how Nebuchadnezzar must have scooted forward on his throne with his mouth hanging open. Then, in one of the most dramatic episodes in the Bible, Daniel recounted Nebuchadnezzar's dream.

> *"You, O king, were looking and behold, there was a single great statue; that statue, which was large and of extraordinary splendor, was standing in front of you, and its appearance was awesome. The head of that statue was made of fine gold, its breast and its arms of silver, its belly and its thighs of bronze, its legs of iron, its feet partly of iron and partly of clay.*
>
> *"You continued looking until a stone was cut out without hands, and it struck the statue on its feet of iron and clay and crushed them. Then the iron, the clay, the bronze, the silver and the gold were crushed all at the same time and became like chaff from the summer threshing floors; and the wind carried them away so that not a trace of them was found. But the stone that struck the statue became a great mountain and filled the whole earth."* (Daniel 2:31–35)

Then without missing a beat, Daniel began to unveil the meaning of the dream.

> *"This was the dream; now we will tell its interpretation before the king. You, O king, are the king of kings, to whom the God of*

heaven has given the kingdom, the power, the strength and the glory; and wherever the sons of men dwell, or the beasts of the field, or the birds of the sky, He has given them into your hand and has caused you to rule over them all. You are the head of gold.

"After you there will arise another kingdom inferior to you, then another third kingdom of bronze, which will rule over all the earth. Then there will be a fourth kingdom as strong as iron; inasmuch as iron crushes and shatters all things, so, like iron that breaks in pieces, it will crush and break all these in pieces. In that you saw the feet and toes, partly of potter's clay and partly of iron, it will be a divided kingdom; but it will have in it the toughness of iron, inasmuch as you saw the iron mixed with common clay. As the toes of the feet were partly of iron and partly of pottery, so some of the kingdom will be strong and part of it will be brittle. And in that you saw the iron mixed with common clay, they will combine with one another in the seed of men; but they will not adhere to one another, even as iron does not combine with pottery.

"In the days of those kings the God of heaven will set up a kingdom which will never be destroyed, and that kingdom will not be left for another people; it will crush and put an end to all these kingdoms, but it will itself endure forever. Inasmuch as you saw

*that a stone was cut out of the mountain
without hands and that it crushed the iron,
the bronze, the clay, the silver and the gold,
the great God has made known to the king
what will take place in the future; so the
dream is true and its interpretation is trustworthy."* (Daniel 2:36–45)

What did all this mean?

The four metals in the great statue represented four great
empires that would appear successively on the world scene to
rule over the civilized world of that day. In the hindsight of history we now know that these four empires were Babylon,
Medo-Persia, Greece, and
Rome. The feet and the ten
toes of iron and clay point
forward, even from our day,
to a final, ten-king form of
the Roman Empire.

The great stone cut out
without hands, which
destroys the great statue, is
Jesus Christ. He will come
at His second coming as a
smiting stone who will
destroy Antichrist and his
kingdom and then set up
His own Kingdom that
will fill the whole earth.

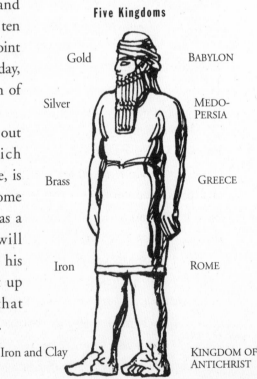

Five Kingdoms

Gold — BABYLON

Silver — MEDO-PERSIA

Brass — GREECE

Iron — ROME

Iron and Clay — KINGDOM OF ANTICHRIST

The Metallic Man of Daniel 2	
World Empire	**Description**
Babylon	Head of gold
Medo-Persia	Chest and arms of silver
Greece	Belly and thighs of bronze
Rome	Legs of iron
Rome II (Antichrist's kingdom)	Feet and ten toes of iron and clay
Christ's kingdom	Stone kingdom that fills the earth

Historically, Nebuchadnezzar and Babylon were the great head of gold on the image. Babylon heads up the list of empires that are opposed to God and His people, Israel.

Babylon, under Nebuchadnezzar, terminated the Davidic kingship and was the first nation to subjugate Jerusalem. The Babylonians came against Jerusalem three times, ultimately destroying the Jewish temple in 586 B.C.

The tale of two cities continues even today. It's still Babylon versus Jerusalem.

The Babylonian empire under Nebuchadnezzar thrived and prospered. He constructed the beautiful hanging gardens for his homesick wife. These became known as one of the Seven Wonders of the Ancient World.

The historian Herodotus visited Babylon about one hundred years after Nebuchadnezzar and reported that he had never in his life seen such a proliferation and abundance of gold. One statue of the god Marduk alone weighed twenty-two tons (that's forty-four thousand pounds!) of solid gold.

Truly, Babylon was the head of gold.

THE JUNGLE BOOK

In Daniel 7, the prophet has a vision at night in which he saw four terrible beasts coming up out of the sea. These four beasts corresponded to the four metals of the image in Daniel 2. Here's the text, summarized in the table immediately following:

In the first year of Belshazzar king of Babylon Daniel saw a dream and visions in his mind as he lay on his bed; then he wrote the dream down and related the following summary of it. Daniel said, "I was looking in my vision by night, and behold, the four winds of heaven were stirring up the great sea.

"And four great beasts were coming up from the sea, different from one another. The first was like a lion and had the wings of an eagle. I kept looking until its wings were plucked, and it was lifted up from the ground and made to stand on two feet like a man; a human mind also was given to it. And behold, another beast, a second one, resembling a bear. And it was raised up on one side, and three ribs were in its mouth between its teeth; and thus they said to it, 'Arise, devour much meat!'

"After this I kept looking, and behold, another one, like a leopard, which had on its back four wings of a bird; the beast also had four heads, and dominion was given to it. After this I kept looking in the night visions,

and behold, a fourth beast, dreadful and terrifying and extremely strong; and it had large iron teeth. It devoured and crushed and trampled down the remainder with its feet; and it was different from all the beasts that were before it, and it had ten horns. While I was contemplating the horns, behold, another horn, a little one, came up among them, and three of the first horns were pulled out by the roots before it; and behold, this horn possessed eyes like the eyes of a man and a mouth uttering great boasts. (Daniel 7:1–8)

The Beasts of Daniel 7

Empire	Description
Babylon	Lion with the wings of an eagle
Medo-Persia	Lopsided bear with three ribs in its mouth
Greece	Leopard with four wings and four heads
Rome	Terrible beast with teeth of iron
Rome II (Antichrist's kingdom)	Ten horns and the little horn

Now consider the obvious parallels between the metals of Daniel 2 and the beasts of Daniel 7:

Parallels Between Daniel 2 and 7		
World Empire	Daniel 2	Daniel 7
Babylon	Head of gold	Lion with the wings of an eagle
Medo-Persia	Chest and arms of silver	Lopsided bear with three ribs in its mouth
Greece	Belly and thighs of bronze	Leopard with four wings and four heads
Rome	Legs of iron	Terrible beast with large iron teeth
Rome II (Antichrist's kingdom)	Feet and ten toes of iron and clay	Ten horns and the little horn

TRANSFER OF POWER

The fact that the Babylonian empire, according to God's plan, was destined to be replaced by another empire lets anyone reading Daniel know that Babylon had to fall. The head of gold had to give way to the chest and arms of silver. The lion had to make room for the bear.

In the fifth chapter of his own book, Daniel describes the transfer of world power from the Babylonian empire to the Medo-Persian empire. On Saturday night, October 12, 539 B.C., Nebuchadnezzar's grandson, Belshazzar, was having a big Babylonian bash. At one point in the feast, in his drunken bravado he ordered the gold vessels that were taken from the temple in Jerusalem almost fifty years earlier to be brought into the hall and filled with wine for his guests. This was a direct affront, a direct challenge, a clear, ill-considered assault on the God of heaven. And Belshazzar got more than he bargained for. Much more.

As he stood near his throne, honoring his false gods and mocking the true God, a heavenly hand suddenly appeared out of nowhere, illumined by the light of the lampstand, and began to write on the plaster of the king's wall. Belshazzar turned ashen and his knees literally began to knock together. "Then the king's face grew pale and his thoughts alarmed him, and his hip joints went slack and his knees began knocking together" (Daniel 5:6).

I would think so!

The divine finger wrote four simple words on the palace wall: MENE, MENE, TEKEL, UPHARSIN.

No one had any idea what these words meant. But someone remembered the old man Daniel, who would have been about eighty years old by this time. Daniel was brought in and delivered God's message of judgment to Belshazzar and Babylon. He rebuked Belshazzar for not learning from his grandfather's punishment (Nebuchadnezzar was made like a beast of the field for seven years—see Daniel 4:1–37). And then, after indicting him for his pride, arrogance, and failure to glorify God, Daniel interpreted the divine hand-writing on the wall.

MENE, MENE	Numbered, Numbered
TEKEL	Weighed
UPHARSIN	Divided

God's message to Belshazzar was as straightforward as a slap across the face. "Belshazzar, your number is up, you do not measure up, and your kingdom is to be broken up."

The night of revelry and revelation turned into a time of retribution.[11] For that very night, the Medo-Persians broke into the city by means of an ingenious plan. The Euphrates River flowed through Babylon, so they dug a huge canal and diverted the water, allowing their soldiers enough room to get under the massive wall. Once the soldiers got under the wall, some helpful soul from the inside (thinking perhaps that they were Babylonian soldiers who had fallen off the wall) opened the gate into the city. The soldiers flooded in and Belshazzar was slain that very night. God's judgment was swift. Babylon's time was up! The kingdom passed to the Medo-Persian empire (see Daniel 5:31).

History's head of gold was finished.

Or was it?

THE REST OF THE STORY

Was the transfer of power in 539 B.C. the end for Babylon? Did Babylon fall, never to rise again? Many people think so. But what does the Bible really say about Babylon? Does the city have a future, even in our day?

It's amazing to me how much space the Bible devotes to describing the downfall and devastation of Babylon. And the fall of Babylon depicted in the Bible, outside the book of Daniel, seems to go far beyond anything that happened in 539 B.C. Far beyond anything that has ever happened to Babylon in the past. Therefore, since this is true, Babylon must rise again. There must be a second coming of Babylon in the end times.

In the next two chapters, let us see what the Bible says about *how* and *when* this New Babylon will meet its final downfall.

CHAPTER FIVE

"FALLEN, FALLEN IS BABYLON THE GREAT!"

No city in human history will ever have such a meteoric rise as New Babylon. Babylon will be rebuilt on the Euphrates River in a relatively short time, as the commercial and economic capital of the world. The world will look on in awe as the city rises from the ashes of time to take her place on the world stage. The New Babylon will shine as one of man's crowning achievements. Man will have done it again. He will have built a city back in Babylon.

But no city in human history will experience such a cataclysmic and total fall as Babylon. God's Word is clear. This city of pride, greed, materialism, and rebellion will face the fierce wrath of almighty God.

JUDGMENT DAY

Several years ago, as I was browsing through a Christian bookstore, I ran across a book called *The Positive Thinker's Bible*. I couldn't resist opening it up to see what it was all about. I immediately noticed that all the "positive" passages in the Bible were highlighted in blue. They were easily identified, so that when you needed a positive message you could find one quickly.

As I thumbed through that Bible, one thing struck me right away. There weren't many blue highlights among the

Old Testament prophets! Now that's not to say that their message is all gloom and doom. The prophets always conclude with a message of bright hope for the future, to motivate God's people to faithfulness in the present. But let's face it—a major strand that runs through the Old Testament prophets is the wrath and judgment of God against sin.

Such a message isn't any more popular today than it was back then. People have never enjoyed hearing about the judgment of God. But God doesn't shy away from it just because it doesn't sit well with man. Through His prophets, God gives the unvarnished, undiluted truth about judgment on those who willfully turn their backs on the King of glory.

Several large segments of the Old Testament deal with God's judgment on nations that forget God. Within these sections, Babylon plays the prominent role. Babylon receives special focus when God begins to judge the nations.

In the New Testament, near the end of the Bible in Revelation 17–18, God again "calls Babylon out" and announces His fierce wrath against the city, its greed, and the false religious system that is centered there.

Let's look briefly at each of these passages so you can see for yourself, from the pages of God's Word, what God says about the final destruction of Babylon.

ISAIAH'S INDICTMENTS

The first place in which Babylon's final fate is foretold is Isaiah 13–14. The Old Testament book of Isaiah contains eleven chapters devoted to God's judgment on the nations surrounding Judah.

The ten specific nations that are listed in Isaiah 13–23 are:

Isaiah's Indictments	
Nation	**Chapter/Verses in Isaiah**
Babylon	13–14
Moab	15–16
Damascus (Syria)	17:1–11
Ethiopia (Cush)	17:12–18:7
Egypt	19–20
Babylon (Persian Gulf area)	21:1–10
Edom	21:11–12
Arabia	21:13–17
Jerusalem	22
Tyre	23

As you can see, Babylon is first on God's "hit list." God even devotes two whole chapters (fifty-four verses) to Babylon. When you read Isaiah 13–14, it seems as if God looks upon Babylon as a kind of prototype, an embodiment of all the nations who rebel against God in pride.

Babylon's destruction is graphically portrayed in Isaiah 13. This might seem a bit long, but I wanted you to get the full flavor of God's displeasure with Babylon, both here and in the other Scriptures that follow:

> *The oracle concerning Babylon which Isaiah the son of Amoz saw. Lift up a standard on the bare hill, raise your voice to them, wave the hand that they may enter the doors of the nobles. I have commanded My consecrated ones, I have even called my mighty warriors, my proudly exulting ones, to execute My anger.*

A sound of tumult on the mountains, like that of many people! A sound of the uproar of kingdoms, of nations gathered together! The LORD of hosts is mustering the army for battle. They are coming from a far country, from the farthest horizons, the LORD and His instruments of indignation, to destroy the whole land.

Wail, for the day of the LORD is near! It will come as destruction from the Almighty. Therefore all hands will fall limp, and every man's heart will melt. They will be terrified, pains and anguish will take hold of them; they will writhe like a woman in labor, they will look at one another in astonishment, their faces aflame. Behold, the day of the LORD is coming, cruel, with fury and burning anger, to make the land a desolation; and He will exterminate its sinners from it.

For the stars of heaven and their constellations will not flash forth their light; the sun will be dark when it rises and the moon will not shed its light. Thus I will punish the world for its evil and the wicked for their iniquity; I will also put an end to the arrogance of the proud and abase the haughtiness of the ruthless. I will make mortal man scarcer than pure gold and mankind than the gold of Ophir.

Therefore I will make the heavens tremble, and the earth will be shaken from its place at the fury of the LORD of hosts in the day of

His burning anger. And it will be that like a hunted gazelle, or like sheep with none to gather them, they will each turn to his own people, and each one flee to his own land. Anyone who is found will be thrust through, and anyone who is captured will fall by the sword.

Their little ones also will be dashed to pieces before their eyes; their houses will be plundered and their wives ravished. Behold, I am going to stir up the Medes against them, who will not value silver or take pleasure in gold. And their bows will mow down the young men, they will not even have compassion on the fruit of the womb, nor will their eye pity children. And Babylon, the beauty of kingdoms, the glory of the Chaldeans' pride, will be as when God overthrew Sodom and Gomorrah.

It will never be inhabited or lived in from generation to generation; nor will the Arab pitch his tent there, nor will shepherds make their flocks lie down there. But desert creatures will lie down there, and their houses will be full of owls; ostriches also will live there, and shaggy goats will frolic there. Hyenas will howl in their fortified towers and jackals in their luxurious palaces. Her fateful time also will soon come and her days will not be prolonged.
(Isaiah 13:1–22)

JUDGMENT IN JEREMIAH

Jeremiah's prophecies of judgment against the nations can be found in Jeremiah 46–52. In his list, Jeremiah saves Babylon's judgment for last. Notice the comparison with Isaiah. Just as Isaiah does, Jeremiah devotes more space and more detail to Babylon's destruction than to that of any other nation—an incredible 110 verses in chapters 50 and 51. Again, Babylon is clearly the focal point of God's wrath.

Here is a list of the seven specific nations that Jeremiah singles out for divine judgment.

Jeremiah's Indictments	
Nation	**Chapter/Verses in Jeremiah**
Egypt	46
Philistia	47
Moab	48
Ammon	49:1–22
Damascus	49:23–33
Elam	49:34–39
Babylon	50–51

Although Jeremiah 50–51 is too lengthy to quote in its entirety, here are some selected sections that reveal the scope and severity of Babylon's fall:

> *The word which the LORD spoke concerning Babylon, the land of the Chaldeans, through Jeremiah the prophet: "Declare and proclaim among the nations. Proclaim it and lift up a standard. Do not conceal it but say, 'Babylon*

has been captured, Bel has been put to shame, Marduk has been shattered; Her images have been put to shame, her idols have been shattered.' For a nation has come up against her out of the north; it will make her land an object of horror, and there will be no inhabitant in it. Both man and beast have wandered off, they have gone away!" (Jeremiah 50:1–3)

"For behold, I am going to arouse and bring up against Babylon a horde of great nations from the land of the north, and they will draw up their battle lines against her; from there she will be taken captive. Their arrows will be like an expert warrior who does not return empty-handed.

"Chaldea will become plunder; all who plunder her will have enough," declares the LORD. "Because you are glad, because you are jubilant, O you who pillage My heritage, because you skip about like a threshing heifer and neigh like stallions, your mother will be greatly ashamed, she who gave you birth will be humiliated. Behold, she will be the least of the nations, a wilderness, a parched land and a desert.

"Because of the indignation of the LORD she will not be inhabited, but she will be completely desolate; everyone who passes by Babylon will be horrified and will hiss because of all her wounds. Draw up your battle lines against

Babylon on every side, all you who bend the bow; shoot at her, do not be sparing with your arrows, for she has sinned against the LORD. Raise your battle cry against her on every side! She has given herself up, her pillars have fallen, her walls have been torn down. For this is the vengeance of the LORD: take vengeance on her; as she has done to others, so do to her.

"Cut off the sower from Babylon and the one who wields the sickle at the time of harvest; from before the sword of the oppressor they will each turn back to his own people and they will each flee to his own land." (Jeremiah 50:9–16)

"I set a snare for you and you were also caught, O Babylon, while you yourself were not aware; you have been found and also seized because you have engaged in conflict with the LORD." The LORD has opened His armory and has brought forth the weapons of His indignation, for it is a work of the Lord GOD of hosts in the land of the Chaldeans.

Come to her from the farthest border; open up her barns, pile her up like heaps and utterly destroy her, let nothing be left to her. Put all her young bulls to the sword; let them go down to the slaughter! Woe be upon them, for their day has come, the time of their punishment. There is a sound of fugitives and refugees from the land of Babylon, to declare in Zion the vengeance of the LORD our God, vengeance for His temple.

"Summon many against Babylon, all those who bend the bow: encamp against her on every side, let there be no escape. Repay her according to her work; according to all that she has done, so do to her; for she has become arrogant against the LORD, against the Holy One of Israel. Therefore her young men will fall in her streets, and all her men of war will be silenced in that day," declares the LORD.

"Behold, I am against you, O arrogant one," declares the Lord GOD of hosts, "For your day has come, the time when I will punish you. The arrogant one will stumble and fall with no one to raise him up; and I will set fire to his cities and it will devour all his environs." (Jeremiah 50:24–32)

"Therefore the desert creatures will live there along with the jackals; the ostriches also will live in it, and it will never again be inhabited or dwelt in from generation to generation. As when God overthrew Sodom and Gomorrah with its neighbors," declares the LORD, "no man will live there, nor will any son of man reside in it.

"Behold, a people is coming from the north, and a great nation and many kings will be aroused from the remote parts of the earth. They seize their bow and javelin; they are cruel and have no mercy. Their voice roars like the sea; and they ride on horses, marshalled like a

man for the battle against you, O daughter of Babylon. The king of Babylon has heard the report about them, and his hands hang limp; distress has gripped him, agony like a woman in childbirth." (Jeremiah 50:39–43)

Suddenly Babylon has fallen and been broken; wail over her! Bring balm for her pain; perhaps she may be healed. We applied healing to Babylon, but she was not healed; forsake her and let us each go to his own country, for her judgment has reached to heaven and towers up to the very skies. The LORD has brought about our vindication; come and let us recount in Zion the work of the LORD our God! (Jeremiah 51:8–10)

"But I will repay Babylon and all the inhabitants of Chaldea for all their evil that they have done in Zion before your eyes," declares the LORD. "Behold, I am against you, O destroying mountain, who destroys the whole earth," declares the LORD, "and I will stretch out My hand against you, and roll you down from the crags, and I will make you a burnt out mountain.

"They will not take from you even a stone for a corner nor a stone for foundations, but you will be desolate forever," declares the LORD. Lift up a signal in the land, blow a trumpet among the nations! Consecrate the nations

against her, summon against her the kingdoms of Ararat, Minni and Ashkenaz; appoint a marshal against her, bring up the horses like bristly locusts.

Consecrate the nations against her, the kings of the Medes, their governors and all their prefects, and every land of their dominion. So the land quakes and writhes, for the purposes of the LORD against Babylon stand, to make the land of Babylon a desolation without inhabitants. The mighty men of Babylon have ceased fighting, they stay in the strongholds; their strength is exhausted, they are becoming like women; their dwelling places are set on fire, the bars of her gates are broken.

One courier runs to meet another, and one messenger to meet another, to tell the king of Babylon that his city has been captured from end to end; the fords also have been seized, and they have burned the marshes with fire, and the men of war are terrified. (Jeremiah 51:24–32)

According to Jeremiah's own book, a copy of Jeremiah 50:1–51:58 was written on a scroll and tied to a rock. After reciting the contents of these two chapters to the Jewish exiles in Babylon, Jeremiah cast it into the Euphrates River (see Jeremiah 51:59–64).

The symbolism is striking. Just as the scroll sank, so Babylon will sink, never to rise again.

WRATH IN REVELATION

No presentation of Babylon's final fall would be complete without the vivid description of Babylon's doom found in Revelation. The book of Revelation unveils the final wrath of God against sin, in preparation for the coming earthly kingdom of Jesus Christ.

It's always been interesting to me that the only end-time city specifically singled out for God's judgment, besides Jerusalem (see Revelation 11:8–13), is Babylon. And this judgment is announced and rehearsed three separate times.

> *And another angel, a second one, followed, saying, "Fallen, fallen is Babylon the great, she who has made all the nations drink of the wine of the passion of her immorality."* (Revelation 14:8)

> *And there were flashes of lightning and sounds and peals of thunder; and there was a great earthquake, such as there had not been since man came to be upon the earth, so great an earthquake was it, and so mighty. The great city was split into three parts, and the cities of the nations fell. Babylon the great was remembered before God, to give her the cup of the wine of His fierce wrath.* (Revelation 16:18–19)

> *After these things I saw another angel coming down from heaven, having great authority, and the earth was illumined with his glory. And he cried out with a mighty voice, saying, "Fallen, fallen is Babylon the great! She has become a*

dwelling place of demons and a prison of every unclean spirit, and a prison of every unclean and hateful bird. For all the nations have drunk of the wine of the passion of her immorality, and the kings of the earth have committed acts of immorality with her, and the merchants of the earth have become rich by the wealth of her sensuality."

I heard another voice from heaven, saying, "Come out of her, my people, so that you will not participate in her sins and receive of her plagues; for her sins have piled up as high as heaven, and God has remembered her iniquities. Pay her back even as she has paid, and give back to her double according to her deeds; in the cup which she has mixed, mix twice as much for her. To the degree that she glorified herself and lived sensuously, to the same degree give her torment and mourning; for she says in her heart, 'I sit as a queen and I am not a widow, and will never see mourning.'

"For this reason in one day her plagues will come, pestilence and mourning and famine, and she will be burned up with fire; for the LORD God who judges her is strong. And the kings of the earth, who committed acts of immorality and lived sensuously with her, will weep and lament over her when they see the smoke of her burning, standing at a distance because of the fear of her torment, saying, 'Woe, woe, the great city, Babylon, the strong city! For

in one hour your judgment has come.' And the merchants of the earth weep and mourn over her, because no one buys their cargoes any more—cargoes of gold and silver and precious stones and pearls and fine linen and purple and silk and scarlet, and every kind of citron wood and every article of ivory and every article made from very costly wood and bronze and iron and marble, and cinnamon and spice and incense and perfume and frankincense and wine and olive oil and fine flour and wheat and cattle and sheep, and cargoes of horses and chariots and slaves and human lives.

"The fruit you long for has gone from you, and all things that were luxurious and splendid have passed away from you and men will no longer find them. The merchants of these things, who became rich from her, will stand at a distance because of the fear of her torment, weeping and mourning, saying, 'Woe, woe, the great city, she who was clothed in fine linen and purple and scarlet, and adorned with gold and precious stones and pearls; for in one hour such great wealth has been laid waste!' And every shipmaster and every passenger and sailor, and as many as make their living by the sea, stood at a distance, and were crying out as they saw the smoke of her burning, saying, 'What city is like the great city?'

"And they threw dust on their heads and were crying out, weeping and mourning, saying,

'Woe, woe, the great city, in which all who had ships at sea became rich by her wealth, for in one hour she has been laid waste!' Rejoice over her, O heaven, and you saints and apostles and prophets, because God has pronounced judgment for you against her." Then a strong angel took up a stone like a great millstone and threw it into the sea, saying, "So will Babylon, the great city, be thrown down with violence, and will not be found any longer. And the sound of harpists and musicians and flute-players and trumpeters will not be heard in you any longer; and no craftsman of any craft will be found in you any longer; and the sound of a mill will not be heard in you any longer; and the light of a lamp will not shine in you any longer; and the voice of the bride-groom and bride will not be heard in you any longer; for your merchants were the great men of the earth, because all the nations were deceived by your sorcery. And in her was found the blood of prophets and of saints and of all who have been slain on the earth."
(Revelation 18:1–24)

Q & A

All this talk about Babylon's destruction raises some questions that I'm sure you are asking at this point. How can Babylon be destroyed if there is no city there to destroy? Does the Bible really say that this destruction will come in the future? What evidence is there in the Bible that Babylon will be rebuilt and destroyed *in the future?* Indeed, what points to the second coming of Babylon?

These are very important questions. Let's see what God's Word has to say about the timing of Babylon's final fall.

CHAPTER SIX

WHEN WILL BABYLON FALL?

When?

That's easily the most difficult question in Bible prophecy.

Most of the time it's not too difficult to figure out *what* the Bible is saying about a certain event, or even *who* is involved. Nor were the prophets of Scripture shy about describing *why*.

But *when* tends to be a different matter. The timing, or chronology, of events is not always so clear.

We have seen in Isaiah 13–14 and Jeremiah 50–51 that God clearly announces the destruction of Babylon by a host of nations. The *who* is clear—it's Babylon. The *what* is clear—Babylon is wiped out. But the question remains: *When did* or *when will* this destruction occur? What destruction of Babylon is Isaiah talking about? Was this a destruction that occurred in his own day? Was he prophesying about the overthrow of Babylon that occurred in 539 B.C., when Babylon fell to the Medo-Persians? Or did Isaiah look far down the road to a destruction of Babylon in the end times?

Let's consider seven important clues or pieces of evidence in Isaiah and Jeremiah that narrow down the time of Babylon's final destruction.

IN THE DAY OF THE LORD

First, in Isaiah 13:6, 9, the Lord gives an indication of the *time* of this event. He says that the destruction will occur in the Day of the Lord.

> *Wail, for the day of the LORD is near! It will come as destruction from the Almighty.... Behold, the day of the LORD is coming, cruel, with fury and burning anger, to make the land a desolation; and He will exterminate its sinners from it.*

The phrase the "day of the LORD" occurs nineteen times in the Old Testament and four times in the New Testament.[12] It refers to any time that God intervenes in human affairs dramatically to bring judgment or blessing. In most cases, however, judgment comes into view, not blessing. Most often, it refers to when God comes down to earth to settle accounts with sinful man.

Some of what we might call "historical days of the Lord" have already occurred. For example, the destruction of Egypt by Nebuchadnezzar in 586 B.C. was called "the day of the LORD" (Ezekiel 30:3, 10). But even when a "near" day of the Lord is in view, the judgment in some way foreshadows, previews, or prefigures the final Day of the Lord in the Great Tribulation (see Joel 2:31; 3:14). In other words, the majority of references to the Day of the Lord look to the future.

SIGNS IN THE HEAVENS

Second, the Lord Himself further narrows down the time. It's clear from the context that this destruction of Babylon will be in the final Day of the Lord during the Tribulation period. Reading a little further in Isaiah 13, we are grabbed by these words:

> *For the stars of heaven and their constellations will not flash forth their light; the sun will be dark when it rises and the moon will not shed its light. Thus I will punish the world for its evil and the wicked for their iniquity; I will also put an end to the arrogance of the proud and abase the haughtiness of the ruthless. I will make mortal man scarcer than pure gold and mankind than the gold of Ophir. Therefore I will make the heavens tremble, and the earth will be shaken from its place at the fury of the LORD of hosts in the day of His burning anger.* (Isaiah 13:10–13)

Nothing even close to this happened in 539 B.C. when Babylon was captured by the Persians. These cosmic disturbances and supernatural signs in the heavens are described elsewhere in the Bible in conjunction with the second coming of Christ to earth.

Later in Isaiah, this same language is used to describe what will happen when Jesus comes back to reign in Jerusalem. "Then the moon will be abashed and the sun ashamed, for the LORD of hosts will reign on Mount Zion and in Jerusalem, and His glory will be before His elders" (Isaiah 24:23).

In Joel's great prophecy of Armageddon, he mentions these same signs.

> *Multitudes, multitudes in the valley of deci-*
> *sion! For the day of the LORD is near in the*
> *valley of decision. The sun and moon grow*
> *dark and the stars lose their brightness. The*
> *LORD roars from Zion and utters His voice*
> *from Jerusalem, and the heavens and the*
> *earth tremble. But the LORD is a refuge for*
> *His people and a stronghold to the sons of*
> *Israel.* (Joel 3:14–16)

In His great sermon on the end times, Jesus actually alludes back to Isaiah 13:10, using this same kind of language to describe what will happen immediately after the Tribulation period in conjunction with His second coming.

> *For just as the lightning comes from the east*
> *and flashes even to the west, so will the coming*
> *of the Son of Man be. Wherever the corpse is,*
> *there the vultures will gather. But immediately*
> *after the tribulation of those days the sun will*
> *be darkened, and the moon will not give its*
> *light, and the stars will fall from the sky, and*
> *the power of the heavens will be shaken, and*
> *then the sign of the Son of Man will appear*
> *in the sky, and then all the tribes of the earth*
> *will mourn, and they will see the Son of Man*
> *coming on the clouds of the sky with power*
> *and great glory.* (Matthew 24:27–30)

Since the destruction of Babylon is described in the same terms as Armageddon and the second coming of Christ, the city will be finally destroyed at the same time.

THE JUDGMENT OF THE WORLD

Third, the time of Babylon's judgment is a time not only for Babylon to face judgment but for all the nations to be judged. Isaiah 13:11–12 says, "Thus I will punish the world for its evil and the wicked for their iniquity; I will also put an end to the arrogance of the proud and abase the haughtiness of the ruthless. I will make mortal man scarcer than pure gold and mankind than the gold of Ophir."

When Babylon is destroyed, God will punish the world for its iniquity. And mankind will be scarcer than gold. Since this has never happened in the past, then it must refer to the future, final judgment of God at the end of the Great Tribulation.

LIKE SODOM AND GOMORRAH

Fourth, Isaiah 13:19 says that when Babylon is finally destroyed, it will be like Sodom and Gomorrah. "Babylon, the beauty of the kingdoms, the glory of the Chaldean's pride, will be as when God overthrew Sodom and Gomorrah."

The prophet Jeremiah says the same thing.

> *Behold, she will be the least of the nations, a wilderness, a parched land and a desert. Because of the indignation of the LORD she will not be inhabited, but she will be completely*

desolate.... Come to her from the farthest bor-
der; open up her barns, pile her up like heaps
and utterly destroy her, let nothing be left to
her.... Therefore the desert creatures will live
there along with the jackals; the ostriches also
will live in it, and it will never be inhabited or
dwelt in from generation to generation. "As
when God overthrew Sodom and Gomorrah
with its neighbors," declares the LORD, "no man
will live there, nor will any son of man reside in
it." (Jeremiah 50:12–13, 26, 39–40)

Isaiah goes on to say that Babylon will be so completely destroyed that the city will never be dwelt in again.

It will never be inhabited or lived in from gen-
eration to generation; nor will the Arab pitch
his tent there, nor will shepherds make their
flocks lie down there. But desert creatures will
lie down there, and their houses will be full of
owls; ostriches also will live there, and shaggy
goats will frolic there. Hyenas will howl in
their fortified towers and jackals in their luxu-
rious palaces. Her fateful time also will soon
come and her days will not be prolonged.
(Isaiah 13:20–22)

In other words, Babylon will be totally wiped out—wiped off the face of the earth.

The question is, did this ever happen in the past? The answer is crystal clear. It didn't. Nothing like this ever happened to the city of Babylon in its long and storied history. Babylon has never been destroyed like this after Jeremiah wrote in about 600 B.C.[13] People continued to live in the city for over a millennium after the prophecies of Isaiah and Jeremiah. Even in modern times, Arabs have pitched their tents in the city.

So you can see this for yourself, let's look at a brief overview of Babylon's history following Judah's return from the seventy-year exile.

| Overview of the History of Babylon ||
Date	Event
539 B.C.	The Persians under King Cyrus conquered Babylon in 539 B.C., but the city wasn't destroyed. The Persians simply captured the city.
450 B.C.	Herodotus, the father of History, visited the city of Babylon. He described it in grand terms. He said the inner walls were 85 feet thick and 340 feet high, with 100 gates. Obviously, at the time of Herodotus, Babylon was still a flourishing city of unbelievable grandeur.
323 B.C.	Alexander the Great visited the city and died there.
312 B.C.	After his death, Alexander's empire was divided among four of his generals. One of those generals, Seleucus, seized Babylon in 312.

| Overview of the History of Babylon ||
Date	Event
25 B.C.	The famous geographer Strabo visited Babylon. He described the Hanging Gardens as one of the Seven Wonders of the Ancient World. He also described the bountiful crops of barley produced in the surrounding country.
A.D. 35	On the day of Pentecost there were Jews in Jerusalem from Babylon (see Acts 2:8–10).
A.D. 64	The apostle Peter wrote his first epistle from Babylon (see 1 Peter 5:13).
A.D. 95	Babylon was still a viable city when the apostle John wrote the book of Revelation. He mentions it in Revelation 17–18.
A.D. 500	The Babylonian Talmud, which was a commentary on the Jewish law, was promulgated from Babylon.

So what does this tell us? It tells us that Babylon has never been destroyed as prophesied by Isaiah and Jeremiah. The city died a long, slow, agonizing death. Even today there are numerous small villages in and around the ancient city. If, then, the prophecies of Babylon's destruction are to be literally fulfilled (as they must be), then they must be referring to a future, catastrophic destruction of Babylon that has not yet occurred. Commenting on Isaiah 13:20–22, prophecy expert John Walvoord says:

As far as the historic fulfillment is concerned, it is obvious from both Scripture and history that these verses have not been literally fulfilled. The city of Babylon continued to flourish after the Medes conquered it, and though its glory dwindled, especially after the control of the Medes and Persians ended in 323 B.C., the city continued in some form or substance until A.D. 1000 and did not experience a sudden termination such as is anticipated in this prophecy.[14]

NO MORE BRICKS

Fifth, the Bible is clear that, when Babylon is destroyed, not one single stone from the city will ever be used in another building project. Jeremiah 51:26 says, "'They will not take from you even a stone for a corner nor a stone for foundations, but you will be desolate forever,' declares the LORD."

The problem is that archaeological discoveries have shown that bricks and stone from ancient Babylon have been repeatedly plundered and reused in later construction projects. Again, the only way for this prophecy to be literally fulfilled is for Babylon to be rebuilt and destroyed once and for all, just as the Bible predicts. When that occurs, none of the bricks from that city will ever be used again.

UNIVERSAL REST AND PEACE

Sixth, the Bible teaches that right after Babylon's destruction, the world will enter into a time of universal rest and peace. Isaiah 14:5–8 describes the scene:

> *The LORD has broken the staff of the wicked, the scepter of rulers which used to strike the peoples in fury with unceasing strokes, which subdued the nations in anger with unrestrained persecution. The whole earth is at rest and is quiet; they break forth into shouts of joy. Even the cypress trees rejoice over you, and the cedars of Lebanon, saying, "Since you were laid low, no more tree cutter comes up against us."*

This time of universal rest looks forward to the time of the Millennium, the one-thousand-year reign of Christ on the earth. It will come only after Babylon is destroyed.

ISRAEL'S FINAL RESTORATION

Seventh, both Isaiah and Jeremiah predict that right after Babylon's destruction, Judah and Israel are restored to the land of Israel and to the Lord in an everlasting covenant. God also says that when Babylon is destroyed, the people of Israel will take their captors captive.

Right after describing Babylon's destruction in Isaiah 13, the prophet goes on to describe what will transpire in the aftermath.

> *When the LORD will have compassion on Jacob*

and again choose Israel, and settle them in their own land, then strangers will join them and attach themselves to the house of Jacob. The peoples will take them along and bring them to their place, and the house of Israel will possess them as an inheritance in the land of the LORD as male servants and female servants; and they will take their captors captive and will rule over their oppressors. And it will be in the day when the LORD gives you rest from your pain and turmoil and harsh service in which you have been enslaved, that you will take up this taunt against the king of Babylon, and say, "How the oppressor has ceased, and how fury has ceased!" (Isaiah 14:1–4)

Jeremiah paints the same picture:

"Declare and proclaim among the nations. Proclaim it and lift up a standard. Do not conceal it but say, 'Babylon has been captured, Bel has been put to shame, Marduk has been shattered; her images have been put to shame, her idols have been shattered....' In those days and at that time," declares the LORD, "the sons of Israel will come, both they and the sons of Judah as well; they will go along weeping as they go, and it will be the LORD their God they will seek. They will ask for the way to Zion, turning their faces in its direction; they will come that they may join themselves to the

LORD in an everlasting covenant that will not be forgotten." (Jeremiah 50:2, 4–5)

Clearly, there has never been a time in the past, after Babylon was destroyed, when the children of Israel and Judah returned to their land, took the Babylonians captive, and joined in an everlasting covenant with the Lord. These texts must therefore refer to the end of the Tribulation period, when Babylon is finally destroyed and the Jewish people are regathered to Israel for the final time, in preparation for the one-thousand-year reign of Christ on earth.

THE FINAL VERDICT: BABYLON MUST BE REBUILT

We have looked at the seven pieces of evidence concerning the time of Babylon's destruction. Here they are in review:

1. Babylon must be destroyed in the Day of the Lord.
2. Babylon's destruction will be accompanied by great signs and wonders in the heavens.
3. Babylon will be destroyed when all the world is judged.
4. Babylon will be destroyed like Sodom and Gomorrah.
5. Babylon will be destroyed so completely that not one brick will be left.
6. Babylon's destruction will usher in a time of world peace.
7. Babylon's destruction will be followed by the regathering and restoration of Israel and

Judah to the land and the Lord in an everlasting covenant.

Based on the evidence, I believe we must conclude that
Babylon will rise again. Since these prophecies must be literally fulfilled, they can only be fulfilled if they refer to a
future city of Babylon that will be rebuilt and destroyed in
the end times.

As Bible teacher Clarence Larkin says:

> The destruction of Sodom and Gomorrah was
> not protracted through many centuries, their
> glory disappeared in a few hours (Gen.
> 19:24–28), and as ancient Babylon was not
> thus destroyed, the prophecies of Isaiah and
> Jeremiah cannot be fulfilled unless there is to be
> a future Babylon that shall be thus destroyed.[15]

Babylon must rise again and be totally wiped out in the
final day of the Lord. There's only one time in man's history
when all this will occur, at the end of the Tribulation in conjunction with the second coming of Jesus Christ. And I
believe what we see happening before our eyes, in Iraq and
the Middle East, is setting the stage for the rapid rise and the
ultimate fall of Babylon.

CHAPTER SEVEN

BABYLON: HOUSE OF EVIL IN THE END TIMES

I n his 2002 State of the Union Address, President George W. Bush made a brief statement that created quite a controversy. He called Iraq, Iran, and North Korea the "axis of evil."

Immediately we heard a massive outcry against his words, for many today seem to object to any notion of evil at all. But I believe that current conditions in our world are leading more and more people to the conclusion that—despite what many have been taught to the contrary—evil truly does exist. Terrible, unimaginable evil.

And it is on the rise.

Of course, the Bible never shies away from speaking the truth. It tells us that evil has existed ever since Satan rebelled against God. When Satan led Adam and Eve into sin, man took his first step downward. From that point on, every person has been born with the same capacity, the same inclination to embrace evil. Since that time, Satan has done everything he can to promote evil and spread its influence far and wide.

It's interesting that the Bible says that, in the end times, evil will be uniquely focused in one geographic location. Where is this place? Is it San Francisco? Las Vegas? Paris?

None of the above. It is Babylon.

God's Word says that, as the end of the age draws near, evil will rear its ugly head again in the place where it began, the city of Babylon on the plain of Shinar.

Perhaps the most amazing prophecy concerning Babylon and end-time evil is found in the ancient prophecy of Zechariah, near the end of the Old Testament.

Let's look at that prediction written more than 2,500 years ago.

ZECHARIAH'S PROPHECY

The Jewish prophet Zechariah was born in Babylon during Judah's seventy-year exile there from 605 B.C. to 536 B.C. He returned to Judah under the leadership of Zerubbabel.

He was one of three Old Testament prophets that God raised up in the days after the exile to call the people to faithfulness. Haggai and Malachi were the other two.

Zechariah's prophecy was given over a two-year period, starting in October 520 B.C. and extending to December 518 B.C. It divides naturally into three main sections.

ZECHARIAH 1–6: EIGHT NIGHT VISIONS (GIVEN ON FEBRUARY 15, 519 B.C.)

1. The Red-Horse Rider Among the Myrtles (1:7–17)
2. The Four Horns and Four Craftsmen (1:18–21)
3. The Surveyor with a Measuring Line (2:1–13)
4. The Cleansing and Crowning of Joshua the High Priest (3:1–10)

5. The Golden Lampstand and Two Olive Trees
   (4:1–14)
6. The Flying Scroll (5:1–4)
7. The Woman in the Ephah (5:5–11)
8. The Four Chariots (6:1–8)

ZECHARIAH 7–8: FOUR MESSAGES (GIVEN ON DECEMBER 7, 518 B.C.)

1. A Message of Rebuke (7:1–7)
2. A Message of Repentance (7:8–14)
3. A Message of Restoration (8:1–17)
4. A Message of Rejoicing (8:18–23)

ZECHARIAH 9–14: TWO BURDENS (ORACLES)

1. Messiah's First Coming to Jerusalem (9–11)
2. Messiah's Second Coming to Jerusalem
   (12–14)

The vision that deals with Babylon in the end times is the seventh vision in the first section—the vision of a woman in a basket.

THE SEVENTH VISION

In verses 5–11 of chapter 5, Zechariah presents the seventh of the eight night visions:

> Then the angel who was talking with me came forward and said, "Look up! Something is appearing in the sky."
> "What is it?" I asked.

He replied, "It is a basket for measuring grain, and it is filled with the sins of everyone throughout the land." When the heavy lead cover was lifted off the basket, there was a woman sitting inside it. The angel said, "The woman's name is Wickedness," and he pushed her back into the basket and closed the heavy lid again. Then I looked up and saw two women flying toward us, with wings gliding on the wind. Their wings were like those of a stork, and they picked up the basket and flew with it into the sky.

"Where are they taking the basket?" I asked the angel.

He replied, "To the land of Babylonia, where they will build a temple for the basket. And when the temple is ready, they will set the basket there on its pedestal." (NLT)

There are five basic keys to understanding this vision:

1. An ephah, or basket, is seen going forth.
2. A woman is in the basket.
3. A lid of lead is on the basket.
4. Two flying women are described as carrying off the basket with the woman in it.
5. The basket is carried to Babylon (Shinar) by the flying women so that a house can be built there for the woman they're carrying inside it.

Let's look briefly at each of these five points so we can understand what this vision is all about.

First, what did Zechariah see? The main thing that Zechariah sees in his vision is "a basket for measuring grain," or an ephah. An ephah was the largest measure in the Old Testament, comprising about ten gallons (1.05 American bushels). It was a dry measure used for measuring flour and barley. The ephah was a symbol for *commerce* or *the economy.*

Second, who did Zechariah see? In this vision he saw a woman in the basket who symbolizes evil or wickedness. Referring to the woman, the angel says, "This is Wickedness!" In other words, the commerce he sees will be *corrupted* or *evil.*

Third, the woman is being held back by something. Interestingly, the wickedness is pushed down into the basket and a heavy lid is closed on top of her. In other words, she is held back in the basket until the time is ready for it to be opened. God is in control. He will not let it out *until He is ready.*

One of the great comforts in studying Bible prophecy is that we see the mighty, sovereign hand of God in control of all things. He controls what happens, how it happens, when it happens, and where it happens.

The holding down or restraining of the woman, who personifies evil, is strikingly similar to the restraining of evil pictured in 2 Thessalonians 2:3–8. In this passage, through Paul, God says that Antichrist cannot be revealed until "the restrainer" is taken out of the way. This restrainer is referred to as both a person and a power.

> *Let no one in any way deceive you, for it will not come unless the apostasy comes first, and the man of lawlessness is revealed, the son of destruction, who opposes and exalts himself*

above every so-called god or object of worship,
so that he takes his seat in the temple of God,
displaying himself as being God. Do you not
remember that while I was still with you, I
was telling you these things? And you know
what restrains him now, so that in his time he
may be revealed. For the mystery of lawlessness
is already at work; only he who now restrains
will do so until he is taken out of the way. And
then that lawless one will be revealed whom
the Lord will slay with the breath of His
mouth and bring to an end by the appearance
of His coming. (2 Thessalonians 2:3–8)

God is telling us that one thing in particular is hindering the full outbreak of evil and opening of the door for Antichrist's entrance onto the world stage. And this hindrance is called the "he who now restrains."

Although there are many popular explanations of the identity of this restrainer, I believe that the restrainer is the Holy Spirit working in and through the church, the body of Christ on earth.[16] When the church is raptured to heaven, the restraint will be removed, and Satan's plans involving Antichrist and the city of Babylon will swing into motion.

Fourth, how is the basket transported? The two women with wings take the basket away.

Some see the two women as demonic forces on an evil mission, seeking to protect the wicked woman and enshrine her for worship.[17] But I believe it's best to identify the women as agent's of God's providence and power, demonstrating that

God is in total control of wickedness. That the two women have wings also seems to indicate that the basket is transported quickly to its new destination.

Fifth, where is the basket taken? Where will this vision be fulfilled? Notice Zechariah's question, "Where are they taking the ephah?" The answer is very specific. "To build a temple for her in the land of Shinar (Babylon)." But this will only occur when everything is ready, Zechariah is told, "and when it is prepared, she will be set there on her own pedestal."

In other words, this will transpire only when everything is ready. Then the basket will be taken to the land of Babylon. After the flood, the first outbreak of evil in the world occurred at Babylon. Everything will come full circle. The world's first capital city will be the place of its final city, Babylon. I believe this means that, in the end times, Babylon will become the world capital of an evil world economic system run by Antichrist.

Henry Morris says, "Zechariah's vision thus clearly foretells a time when the center of world finance and commerce will be removed from its bases in New York and Geneva and other great cities and transported quickly across the world to a new foundation and headquarters in the land of Shinar. The land of Shinar, of course, is simply a biblical term for Babylon, and has been ever since Babel was first erected there."[18]

The return of wickedness to its place of origin in Babylon will set the stage for God's final judgment on Babylon, as recorded in Isaiah 13–14, Jeremiah 50–51, and Revelation 17–18.

GETTING THE PICTURE?

I hope by now that the Bible's teaching about Babylon is beginning to sound like a familiar refrain. Many people never realize that the Bible has so much to say about this city. Zechariah 5 is just one more piece to the puzzle. It contains the final mention of Babylon in the Old Testament, and it tells us that God isn't through with her.

We aren't finished yet, either. One final piece to the puzzle must be put into place.

Babylon figures prominently in the book of Revelation. Here, God gives us His *final word* about Babylon's place in the end times.

CHAPTER EIGHT

BABYLON IN REVELATION 17–18

T he Book of Revelation is a majestic, moving, Messianic book. Revelation tells us about the judgments of the coming Tribulation period; the Antichrist; the Second Coming of Christ to earth; the one-thousand-year reign of Christ; the Great White Throne Judgment; the new heaven; the new earth; and the heavenly city, New Jerusalem.

It might surprise you, however, to know what topic or event receives the most attention in Revelation. If you guessed Babylon, you guessed right!

The book of Revelation contains 404 verses, and forty-two of these verses deal with Babylon (see Revelation 17–18). When you add in Revelation 14:8 and 16:19, which also speak of Babylon's future, the total number of verses dealing with Babylon increases to forty-four. That's 11 percent of the entire book of Revelation devoted to one subject: Babylon.

Think about that. In the final book of the Bible, God's great apocalypse, or unveiling of the future, one out of every nine verses concerns Babylon. Obviously, Babylon retains a key place in the mind of God, and in His final plan for the ages.

Let's look together to see what Revelation teaches us about the second coming of Babylon.

A PREVIEW OF COMING ATTRACTIONS

The heart of Revelation is the fourteen chapters contained in Revelation 6–19. These fourteen chapters give a gripping overview of the key events and players in the final drama of the ages, the seven-year Tribulation period.

I like to call Revelation 14 a preview of coming attractions. It gives six brief vignettes, or snapshots, of events that are coming later in Revelation. One of these previews concerns the destruction of Babylon.

> *And another angel, a second one, followed, saying, "Fallen, fallen is Babylon the great, she who has made all the nations drink of the wine of the passion of her immorality." Then another angel, a third one, followed them, saying with a loud voice, "If anyone worships the beast and his image, and receives a mark on his forehead or on his hand, he also will drink of the wine of the wrath of God, which is mixed in full strength in the cup of His anger; and he will be tormented with fire and brimstone in the presence of the holy angels and in the presence of the Lamb.* (Revelation 14:8–10)

We hear more about Babylon in Revelation 16:18–21:

> *And there were flashes of lightning and sounds and peals of thunder; and there was a great earthquake, such as there had not been since man came to be upon the earth, so great an earthquake was it, and so mighty. The great*

*city was split into three parts, and the cities of
the nations fell. Babylon the great was remembered before God, to give her the cup of the
wine of His fierce wrath. And every island
fled away, and mountains were not found.
And huge hailstones, about one hundred
pounds each, came down from heaven upon
men; and men blasphemed God because of the
plague of the hail, because its plague was
extremely severe.*

This mention of Babylon introduces us to the final
description of this great city in Revelation 17–18.

BABYLON IN REVELATION 17–18

Babylon's featured appearance in Revelation occurs in
chapters 17–18. Here, the book of Revelation describes in
dramatic detail the rise and fall of New Babylon.

Many scholars and Bible teachers have identified
Babylon as other than the literal city of Babylon. It has been
variously identified as Rome, New York City, the United
States, the Vatican (Roman Catholic church), and Jerusalem,
to mention just a few of the more prominent candidates.

I believe the references to Babylon in Revelation 17–18
refer to a literal, rebuilt city of Babylon in modern-day Iraq
on the Euphrates river, which God will destroy at the end of
the Tribulation. Let me list the *nine major points* that favor
this identification.

"BABYLON" MEANS BABYLON

First, Revelation is filled with the names of many geographic places: Ephesus, Smyrna, Pergamum, Thyatira, Sardis, Philadelphia, Laodicea, Patmos (see Revelation 2–3). These names are almost universally understood as the literal locations their names denote. Armageddon, as mentioned in Revelation 16:16, is a literal place in northern Israel.

The one time John wants to identify a location using symbolic language, he alerts the reader to the fact that it is non-literal. In Revelation 11:8, he refers to Jerusalem as "Sodom and Egypt," but he makes it clear that he is not speaking literally: "The great city which mystically is called Sodom and Egypt." John is being very careful here to let the reader know when he is not speaking literally of a geographic location. That leads me to believe that when he leaves explanations of this sort out, he intends for us to take his words at face value.

In Revelation, the great city is specifically called "Babylon" six times (see 14:8; 16:19; 17:5; 18:2, 10, 21). Although it might be possible that the name "Babylon" is a code name for Rome, New York City, Jerusalem, or some other city, there is no such indication in the text. And since the Bible itself doesn't imply that the term ought to be taken figuratively or symbolically, it is far safer to take it as referring to literal Babylon.

Henry Morris supports this literal understanding of Babylon. "It must be stressed again that *Revelation* means 'unveiling,' not 'veiling.' In the absence of any statement in the context to the contrary, therefore, we must assume that the term Babylon applies to the real city of Babylon, although it also may extend far beyond that to the whole system centered at Babylon as well."[19]

IN THE WILDERNESS

Second, in Revelation 17:3 we read that the woman, identified as Babylon, was out in the wilderness. "And he carried me away in the Spirit into a wilderness; and I saw a woman sitting on a scarlet beast." The mention of the wilderness is probably an allusion to the "oracle concerning the wilderness of the sea" in Isaiah 21:1 which includes the statement, "Fallen, fallen is Babylon" (Isaiah 21:9). The wilderness of the sea is a reference to the sandy wastes or sea country in the Persian Gulf area, outside of Babylon on the Euphrates.

This is a clear link between Babylon in Revelation 17 and the literal city of Babylon in the Old Testament.

DANIEL CONTINUED

Third, while Daniel is not the most frequently quoted Old Testament book in Revelation, I believe it is the one that most influenced the apostle John. Revelation 4–22 is almost a continuation of Daniel. It's like the sequel; in a sense it could be called "Daniel, Part Two." So let's check it out: When Daniel mentions Babylon, what does he mean?

Literal Babylon, of course.

If Daniel is the key background book for Revelation, then what should we assume *Babylon* means in Revelation unless told otherwise? It has to mean *literal Babylon.*

SATAN'S CITY

Fourth, as we have already seen, Babylon is the most mentioned city in the Bible, behind Jerusalem. Babylon is referred to about three hundred times. And throughout

Scripture, Babylon is pictured as the epitome of evil and rebellion against God. Babylon is Satan's capital city on earth.

1. Babylon is the city where man first began to worship himself in organized rebellion against God (see Genesis 11:1–11).
2. Babylon was the capital city of the first world ruler, Nimrod (see Genesis 10:8–10; 11:9).
3. Nebuchadnezzar, king of Babylon, destroyed the city of Jerusalem and the temple in 586 B.C.
4. Babylon was the capital city of the first of four Gentile world empires to rule over Jerusalem.

Since Babylon was the capital city of the first world ruler and is pictured as Satan's capital city on earth throughout Scripture, it makes sense that in the end times, he will once again raise up this city as the capital city of the final world ruler. In Charles Dyer's excellent, bestselling book, *The Rise of Babylon,* he says, "Throughout history, Babylon has represented the height of rebellion and opposition to God's plans and purposes, so God allows Babylon to continue during the final days. It is almost as though he 'calls her out' for a final duel. But this time, the conflict between God and Babylon ends decisively. The city of Babylon will be destroyed."[20]

LOCATION, LOCATION, LOCATION

Fifth, the city of Babylon on the Euphrates fits the criteria for this city as described in Revelation 17–18. Henry Morris highlights the advantages of Babylon as a world capital:

> Nevertheless, Babylon is indeed a prime
> prospect for rebuilding, entirely apart from

any prophetic intimations. Its location is the most ideal in the world for any kind of international center. Not only is it in the beautiful and fertile Tigris-Euphrates plain, but it is near some of the world's richest oil reserves.

Computer studies for the Institute of Creation Research have shown, for example, that Babylon is very near the geographical center of all the earth's land masses. It is within navigable distances to the Persian Gulf and is at the crossroads of the three great continents of Europe, Asia, and Africa.

Thus there is no more ideal location anywhere for a world trade center, a world communications center, a world banking center, a world educational center, or especially, a world capital! The greatest historian of modern times, Arnold Toynbee, used to stress to all his readers and hearers that Babylon would be the best place in the world to build a future world cultural metropolis.

With all these advantages, and with the head start already made by the Iraqis, it is not far-fetched to suggest that the future capital of the 'United Nations Kingdom,' the ten-nation federation established at the beginning of the Tribulation, should be established there.[21]

THE RIVER EUPHRATES

Sixth, the Euphrates River is mentioned by name twice in Revelation (9:14; 16:12). In Revelation 9:14, the text tells us that four fallen angels are being held at the Euphrates River, awaiting the appointed time for them to lead forth a host of demons to destroy one-third of mankind. In Revelation 16:12, the sixth bowl judgment is poured out and dries up the Euphrates River to prepare the way for the kings of the east. These references to the Euphrates point to the fact that something important and evil is occurring there. The rebuilt city of Babylon on the Euphrates, functioning as a great commercial and political center for Antichrist, is a good explanation for this emphasis on the Euphrates River in Revelation.

TWO WICKED WOMEN

Seventh, as we have already seen, Zechariah 5:5–11 records an incredible vision that pertains to the city of Babylon in the last days.

> *Then the angel who was talking with me came forward and said, "Look up! Something is appearing in the sky."*
>
> *"What is it?" I asked.*
>
> *He replied, "It is a basket for measuring grain, and it is filled with the sins of everyone throughout the land." When the heavy lead cover was lifted off the basket, there was a woman sitting inside it. The angel said, "The woman's name is Wickedness," and he pushed her back into the basket and closed the heavy lid again. Then I looked up and saw two women flying toward us, with wings gliding on the wind.*

> *Their wings were like those of a stork, and they*
> *picked up the basket and flew with it into the sky.*
> *"Where are they taking the basket?" I asked*
> *the angel.*
> *He replied, "To the land of Babylonia,*
> *where they will build a temple for the basket.*
> *And when the temple is ready, they will set the*
> *basket there on its pedestal."* (NLT)

As we have already seen, the prophet Zechariah, writing in about 520 B.C., twenty years after the fall of Babylon to the Medo-Persians, saw evil returning to its original place in Babylon in the future. In this vision, Zechariah sees a woman who is named "Wickedness." Then he sees this woman carried away in a basket in the last days to the land of Babylon, where a temple will be built for her.

Note the parallels in the chart below.

| Parallels between Zechariah 5:5–11 & Revelation 17–18 ||
Zechariah 5:5–11	Revelation 17–18
Woman sitting in a basket	Woman sitting on the beast, seven mountains, and many waters (17:3, 9, 15)
Emphasis on commerce (a basket for measuring grain)	Emphasis on commerce (merchant of grain, 18:13)
Woman's name is Wickedness	Woman's name is Babylon the Great, Mother of Harlots and of the Abominations of the Earth
Focus on false worship (a temple is built for the woman)	Focus on false worship (17:5)
Woman is taken to Babylon	Woman is called Babylon

God's Word teaches that, in the end times, wickedness will again rear its ugly head in the same place where it began—Babylon. John's prostitute will fulfill Zechariah 5:5–11, as Babylon is established as the last-days economic world capital that embodies evil.

Revelation 18:10–18 lists the twenty-nine things that Babylon trades as the center of world commerce.

> *"Woe, woe, the great city, Babylon, the strong city! For in one hour your judgment has come."*
> *And the merchants of the earth weep and mourn over her, because no one buys their cargoes any more; cargoes of gold and silver and precious stones and pearls and fine linen and purple and silk and scarlet, and every kind of citron wood and every article of ivory and every article made from very costly wood and bronze and iron and marble, and cinnamon and spice and incense and perfume and frankincense and wine and olive oil and fine flour and wheat and cattle and sheep, and cargoes of horses and chariots and slaves and human lives. And the fruit you long for has gone from you, and all things that were luxurious and splendid have passed away from you and men will no longer find them. The merchants of these things, who became rich from her, will stand at a distance because of the fear of her torment, weeping and mourning, saying, "Woe, woe, the great city, she who was clothed in fine linen and purple and scarlet, and adorned with gold*

*and precious stones and pearls; for in one hour
such great wealth has been laid waste!" And
every shipmaster and every passenger and sailor,
and as many as make their living by the sea,
stood at a distance, and were crying out as they
saw the smoke of her burning, saying, "What
city is like the great city?"*

Babylon is portrayed here as the commercial center of
the whole world . . . and great is its collapse!

THE DESTRUCTION OF BABYLON

Eighth, as we have already noted, the city of Babylon was
never destroyed suddenly and completely as is predicted in
Isaiah 13–14 and Jeremiah 50–51. The statements concerning Babylon's destruction in Revelation 17–18 are conspicu-
ously similar to the description of her doom in these Old
Testament passages. This leads me to believe that the same
city is the subject of all these passages.

BABYLON IN PAIRS

Ninth, chapters 50 and 51 of Jeremiah serve as a kind of
Old Testament counterpart to Revelation 17–18. Jeremiah
50–51 clearly describes the city of Babylon on the
Euphrates. As shown in the chart below, the many parallels between this passage and the future Babylon in
Revelation 17–18 indicate that they are both describing
the same city.

Parallels Between Babylon in Jeremiah 50–51 and Revelation 17–18 [22]		
Description of Babylon	Jeremiah 50–51	Revelation 17–18
Compared to a golden cup	51:7	17:3–4; 18:6
Dwelling on many waters	51:13	17:1
Involved with nations	51:7b	17:2
Named the same	50:1	18:10
Destroyed suddenly	51:8	18:8
Destroyed by fire	51:30	17:16
Never to be inhabited	50:39	18:21
Punished according to her works	50:29	18:6
Fall illustrated	51:63–64	18:21
God's people flee	51:6, 45	18:4
Heaven rejoices	51:48	18:20

Someone has said that the Book of Revelation is "the Grand Central Station of the Bible—because it's where all the trains of thought in the whole Bible come in." That's exactly what we have seen. In Revelation 17–18, Babylon's train comes in.

THE TWO BABYLONS

As we have already observed, from the time of Genesis 10–11, the word *Babylon* has represented both a city and the religious system that arose in that city. Babylon is a literal geographical location on the Euphrates river. But it is also the false religious system that began at the tower of Babel when, for the first time, men came together and organized their own religion in rebellion against God. That false religion spread out from there to all the other major nations of the earth and still affects us today. For example, how many millions of people still read horoscopes based on Babylonian astrological charts?

It appears that Babylon in its final form in Revelation 17–18 is again a system and a city. The location is clearly the same in both Revelation 17 and 18. It's the city of New Babylon. However, two different aspects of the same city are in view in Revelation 17 and 18. These two aspects share the same geographical headquarters.

REVELATION 17—RELIGIOUS BABYLON

The focus in Revelation 17 is on Babylon in its religious character, climaxing in a world religion in the first three and one-half years of the Tribulation. Babylon in Revelation 17 is a false religious system centered in Babylon. The major focus of the indictment of Babylon in Revelation 17 is on the city's abominations, or spiritual idolatry (see 17:4–5).

The harlot is identified as:

> "BABYLON THE GREAT, THE
> MOTHER OF HARLOTS AND OF THE
> ABOMINATIONS OF THE EARTH."

Babylon is the mother, the source, the polluted fountain from which all spiritual harlotry flows. This takes us all the way back to the tower of Babel.

After the rapture of all true believers to heaven, the great religious system that began in Babylon after the flood will come to the forefront again. Man will again organize in rebellion against the Creator, just as he did at the tower of Babel.

Babylon is pictured as a great harlot. I believe this pictures the spiritual harlotry of the city and represents an ecclesiastical or religious entity that is a counterfeit of the true.

Arnold Fruchtenbaum identifies Babylon the harlot in Revelation 17:

> Babylon the Harlot represents the one-world religious system that rules over the religious affairs during the first half of the Tribulation. She rules over the nations of the world (the many waters) fully controlling the religious affairs and has the reluctant support of the government. The headquarters of this one world religion will be the rebuilt city of Babylon, the "mother" of idolatry, for it was here that idolatry and false religion began (Genesis 11:1–9).[23]

In prophetic Scripture, prostitution, fornication, and adultery are frequently associated with idolatry or false religion (see Isaiah 23:15–17; Jeremiah 2:20–31; 13:27; Ezekiel 16:17–19; Hosea 2:5; Nahum 3:4). New Babylon is the epitome of spiritual harlotry, fornication, and idolatry.

As Robert Thomas, an expert on Revelation, says, "She leads the world in the pursuit of false religion whether it be paganism or perverted revealed religion. She is the symbol for a system that reaches back to the tower of Babel (Gen. 10:9–10; 11:1–9) and extends into the future when it will peak under the regime of the beast."[24]

REVELATION 18—COMMERCIAL BABYLON

Revelation 18:1 begins with the words, "After these things." In Revelation these words generally signal something new being introduced (see Revelation 4:1).

I believe that in Revelation 18 this phrase signals a shift or change in focus from Babylon in its religious aspect, in the first half of the seven-year Tribulation, to its economic, commercial, and political aspect that dominates the world in the last half of the Tribulation.

As one reads Revelation 18, it becomes clear that Babylon is the center of economic power. The city is connected with the merchants of the earth (see 18:3, 11, 15, 23) and those who are engaged in maritime commerce (see 18:17). The long list of goods and cargo associated with Babylon marks the city out as an economic juggernaut (see 18:11–13).

The guilt of Babylon in chapter 18 primarily stems from her sensuality, which is associated with materialism and wanton luxury.

FUTURE TENSE

The city of New Babylon will be rebuilt in Iraq in the last days. It will boast two different aspects that will bring the world under its sway. The city will be home to a great religious system pictured as a prostitute in Revelation 17 and to a great economic, commercial, and political center for the Antichrist's empire described in Revelation 18.

Wickedness will return to this place for its final stand. As John Walvoord says, "The end times bring together these two major lines of truth about Babylon and indicate God's final judgment on it."[25]

The rise of Iraq in recent years on the world's political and economic scene, because of her huge revenues from oil, is not an accident. In spite of the Gulf War and tremendous worldwide pressure, Iraq remains a formidable foe. This current rebuilding and rise of Babylon is a key part of God's plan for the last days.

CHAPTER NINE

ANTICHRIST: KING OF BABYLON

T he logistics alone are incredible, the cost, the... everything."

"What?"

"He wants to move the U.N."

"Move it?"

Steve nodded.

"Where?"

"It sounds stupid."

"Everything sounds stupid these days," Bailey said.

"He wants to move it to Babylon."

"You're not serious."

"*He* is."

"I hear they've been renovating that city for years. Millions of dollars invested in making it, what, New Babylon?"

"Billions."[26]

In the bestselling Left Behind series, the Antichrist, Nicolae Carpathia, rules the world from his headquarters in a city called New Babylon. It's the rebuilt city of Babylon in modern Iraq. While the Left Behind series is fictional, it is based on God's blueprint for the end times in the Bible. And the rebuilding of New Babylon as the Antichrist's commercial, political headquarters is anything but a fable.

The Bible explicitly links the final world ruler to the ancient city of Babylon. According to God's Word, Satan's city will rise again to be ruled over by one man, one last time. The book of Revelation pictures Antichrist as the ruler of the whole world.

Antichrist is the king of Babylon.

BABYLON AND THE BEAST

In Revelation, the great city of Babylon and the Antichrist are closely associated with one another. This connection first becomes clear in Revelation 14:8–10:

> *And another angel, a second one, followed, saying, "Fallen, fallen is Babylon the great, she who has made all the nations drink of the wine of the passion of her immorality." Then another angel, a third one, followed them, saying with a loud voice, "If anyone worships the beast and his image, and receives a mark on his forehead or on his hand, he also will drink of the wine of the wrath of God, which is mixed in full strength in the cup of His anger; and he will be tormented with fire and brimstone in the presence of the holy angels and in the presence of the Lamb."*

In these verses the doom of Babylon entails the doom of those who worship the beast, or Antichrist.

BEAUTY ON THE BEAST

In Revelation 17:3–6, the close relationship between Babylon and the Beast becomes even clearer. Here the city of Babylon is portrayed as a gaudy prostitute riding on the back of the scarlet beast, which pictures the Antichrist and his end-time empire.

> *And he carried me away in the Spirit into a wilderness; and I saw a woman sitting on a scarlet beast, full of blasphemous names, having seven heads and ten horns. The woman was clothed in purple and scarlet, and adorned with gold and precious stones and pearls, having in her hand a gold cup full of abominations and of the unclean things of her immorality, and on her forehead a name was written, a mystery, "BABYLON THE GREAT, THE MOTHER OF HARLOTS AND OF THE ABOMINATIONS OF THE EARTH." And I saw the woman drunk with the blood of the saints, and with the blood of the witnesses of Jesus. When I saw her, I wondered greatly.* (Revelation 17:3–6)

As you might imagine, John's curiosity was piqued after seeing this vision—and the apostle's angel guide was willing to explain. "And the angel said to me, 'Why do you wonder? I will tell you the mystery of the woman and the beast that carries her, which has the seven heads and ten horns'" (Revelation 17:7).

The rest of Revelation 17 is the interpretation of what John saw. The meaning of the beast is interpreted in 17:8;

the seven heads in 17:9–11; the ten horns in 17:12–17; and the woman in 17:18.

But one thing is sure from this vision: Whatever the woman and the beast represent, they are very closely tied together. Beauty is riding on the beast.

Her riding the beast indicates that she controls him in some way or exercises strong influence over him. Their relationship is one of both convenience and necessity.

I believe that the scarlet beast with seven heads and ten horns is the Antichrist and his ten-kingdom empire, as described in detail in Daniel 7 and Revelation 13. The harlot in Revelation 17 represents the false religious system, centered in the city of Babylon, which gives spiritual cohesion to the system.[27]

THE RISE OF ANTICHRIST

The Bible tells us that when Antichrist begins his ascent to power he will rise from within a reunited ten-kingdom form of the Roman Empire. The first unmistakable reference to Antichrist in the Bible is in Daniel 7:8, where he is called "the little horn" that arises among the ten horns on a terrible beast representing the reformulated Roman Empire.

The ten horns on the beast represent ten kings, or leaders, who rule simultaneously. These ten horns on this fourth beast correspond to the ten toes on the image in King Nebuchadnezzar's dream in Daniel 2.

But there is a problem with this picture.

We know from history that the Roman Empire has never existed in a ten-kingdom form. It has never been ruled over by ten kings. For this reason, I believe this passage must be speaking of a final form of the Roman Empire that will be reunited in the end times—and that will be ruling the world when Jesus returns.

When you think about it, unlike the other empires before it, the Roman empire was never destroyed and replaced by another empire. It simply fell apart. But in the end times, the Bible teaches that it will be reunited or revived in a form that will be ruled initially by ten kings, or powerful rulers. But at some point "the little horn" will push his way up among them and take total control.

Since this is true, the reuniting of the Roman Empire is one of the key signs of the times. As we approach the end, we should begin to see a reconstitution, revival, or reuniting of the core nations of the historical Roman Empire.

And that is exactly what we see happening today.

It's incredible! The stage is being set right before our eyes for what Daniel predicted over 2,500 years ago.

THE EUNITING OF THE ROMAN EMPIRE

Beginning in 1957, the nations of Europe began to come together, one by one, into an economic and political union. That union has gone through various stages and names. But today is known simply as the EU—the European Union.

At present, the EU consists of fifteen nations. Leaders in Europe, however, are hailing the creation of a new European Union, uniting twenty five countries that stretch from Ireland to the Aegean Sea.

The new agreement to add ten new members is being called Europe's "biggest political union since the Roman Empire—and the first made by the free will of its members."[28]

The ten new members are slated to join on May 1, 2004. They include Poland, the Czech Republic, Hungary, Slovenia, Cyprus, Malta, Slovakia, Latvia, Lithuania, and Estonia. Two more nations, Romania and Bulgaria, could join in 2007.

Here is how the population of the EU compares to the United States at its various stages:[29]

Current U.S. population	281.4 million
Current EU—15 nations	375.3 million
25-nation form of the EU	450.5 million
27-nation form of the EU	481.2 million

According to EU officials, the present EU represents nothing more than Act I. In Act II a new constitution will be necessary, which is due by the middle of 2003. Some of the issues that are being considered are: Should there be more centralized decision making? Does Europe need an elected president?

On January 1, 2002, the Euro became the official single currency of the EU. At present it has been adopted by twelve of the fifteen member nations. When the currency became official, a CNN report said, "For the first time since the Roman Empire, a large portion of Europe now shares a common currency."[30]

It's only a matter of time until all the nations of Europe use the Euro. Economically, this will bring them together to a point of no return. It is inconceivable that any of the nations could extract themselves after becoming a part of this economic union.

It's easy to see how all of these developments are paving the way for one man to come on the scene and take control of the EU. More centralized authority, greater economic dependency, and an elected president of Europe would set the stage perfectly for the rise of Antichrist.

It doesn't seem like that day could be very far away.

WHY REBUILD BABYLON?

Another question that we might be tempted to ask at this point is, "Why rebuild Babylon?" Why would Antichrist—or anyone else—want to rebuild the city? What motivation could there be?

Although no one can answer this question with certainty, there are several plausible answers. We will discuss these in more detail in chapter 12, but for now suffice it to say that Antichrist will be led to build this city—or to improve upon the building already begun—for political and commercial reasons.

Babylon is in the center of a huge percentage of the world's oil wealth and is a strategic military location between the East and the West.

Harold Willmington, a noted expert in end-time prophecy, says:

> But what purpose or purposes might be served by the rebuilding of Babylon? Several could be listed. As God has placed his name and associated his presence upon a certain location, the city of Jerusalem (see 1 Kings 8:29; 11:36; 15:4), it seems not unreasonable that Satan may do the same—upon the city of Babylon.

Beyond this consideration, a rebuilt Babylon could serve as a natural geographical location for the Antichrist's capital headquarters. Babylon is located on the Euphrates River. This mighty body of water always marked the boundary between eastern and western empires in ancient days. From this city the Antichrist may attempt to unite the powers of the East (China, Japan, India, etc.) with his ten-nation western empire.[31]

SYMBOL OF POWER

Antichrist may also locate his headquarters in this city for symbolic reasons.

Sometimes literal places can also become symbolic of some characteristic or emotion. For instance, Waterloo is a literal place but it symbolizes utter defeat. Armageddon is a place in northern Israel, yet it has come to symbolize a total, conclusive conflict. Las Vegas is a real city, and it has come to symbolize sin and decadence.

Likewise, the name *Babylon* refers to a literal place, but the word also evokes notions of intrigue, mystery, pleasure, and power. In *Webster's New Collegiate Dictionary,* Babylon is defined as "a city devoted to materialism and the pursuit of sensual pleasure."[32] (I couldn't help but notice that the aging rock band, The Rolling Stones, entitled one of their recent tours Bridges to Babylon.)

In the early church it was widely believed that the Antichrist would be born in the ancient city of Babylon on the Euphrates.[33] This city was so associated with evil that it was seen as the perfect place for the man of sin to get his start.

Many people are unaware that Babylon is also the place where Alexander the Great died in 323 B.C., intending to make it his eastern capital. Napoleon also had plans to rebuild Babylon. In the French Department of War in Paris, there are records of surveys and maps of Babylon made by Napoleon. It is believed that he intended to rebuild the ancient city into a "New Babylon," making it his capital in recognition of its strategic position as a governmental and commercial center.[34]

The symbolism of Antichrist establishing or enlarging a city called New Babylon would be incredible. Antichrist could put his eastern capital there just as Alexander the Great attempted to do, and he could build the city Napoleon only dreamed of. He could also make both a real and a symbolic showing of his power over the world economy by controlling the main oil fields of the world.

SIGNPOSTS OF THE END TIMES

The Bible says that, in the end times, the city of Babylon will ride on the back of the Antichrist and his reunited, ten-kingdom form of the Roman Empire. It's incredible today that we see both of these signs on the horizon, converging at the same time. This is exactly what we should expect if the coming of Christ is near.

The current EU is not the fulfillment of the reunited Roman Empire. It does not exist in a ten-king/kingdom form as prophesied in Scripture. And current events in Iraq are not fulfilling any specific biblical prophecies. What we see in Iraq and Europe today, however, certainly does point toward the biblical prediction for Babylon and Europe in the end times.

That we see the rise of Babylon and the reuniting of the Roman Empire both taking shape on the same stage, at the same time, should encourage us to believe that the coming of Christ could be very near.

In the words of Jesus, "right at the door."

CHAPTER TEN

IRAQ AND THE COMING ISLAMIC INVASION OF ISRAEL

Without question, Iraq is one of the key players in the Middle East/Persian Gulf area today. Saddam Hussein has consistently tried to position himself to lead the Muslim/Arab world, as a latter-day Arab hero in the image of King Nebuchadnezzar.

He was also an enormous admirer of the greatest pan-Arab leader of modern times, Egyptian leader Gamal Abdel Nasser. That's why Saddam joined the strongly nationalistic Baath Arab Socialist Party. When a new Baath party government was formed in 1968, Saddam assumed leadership roles and became president in 1979 after shoving aside his ailing predecessor.

Saddam has consistently tried to galvanize the Arab world under his leadership. In the 1980s he went to war with Iran in a long, costly campaign in which an estimated one million people died. Saddam hated the Iranians, who are descended from the ancient Persians. His hatred roots all the way back to 539 B.C., when the Persians conquered Babylon.

In 1990 he tried to "annex" Kuwait, maintaining that this neighboring nation is part of the ancient land of Babylon. His forces invaded, conquered, and plundered defenseless Kuwait, stopping only when a coalition of nations intervened, led by the U.S. and Britain.

But more than anything else, Saddam has hated Israel.

When Saddam became president, he republished a tract authored by his uncle Tulfah, who was governor of Baghdad. The tract was titled *Three Whom God Should Not Have Created: Persians, Jews, and Flies.*

Saddam took every opportunity during the Gulf War to lob Scud missiles into Israel. He nurses an insane desire to conquer Israel and the Jews, as his hero, Nebuchadnezzar, did in the sixth century B.C.

In 1967, prior to Saddam's rise to power, Iraq invaded Israel in concert with the other Arab nations and gave aid to Syria when the Syrians invaded Israel again in 1973.

But all of this raises a very important question for anyone who has studied Bible prophecy. *Why doesn't Iraq join the Islamic confederation of nations when they invade Israel in the end times?* Why is Iraq conspicuous by its absence in the end-time invasion of Israel.

To answer this question, we need to take a brief look at Ezekiel 38–39, which details the coming Islamic invasion of Israel.

GOG AND MAGOG

Ezekiel 38–39 predicts that a massive confederation of nations will invade the land of Israel in the latter years, while Israel is enjoying a time of great peace and prosperity. The prophet Ezekiel wrote these chapters more than 2,500 years ago, yet they read like today's headlines.

Ezekiel specifically listed the precise alliance of nations

that will invade Israel in the latter years, or end times. The list is found in Ezekiel 38:1–6:

> *And the word of the LORD came to me saying, "Son of man, set your face toward Gog of the land of Magog, the prince of Rosh, Meshech and Tubal, and prophesy against him and say, 'Thus says the Lord GOD, "Behold, I am against you, O Gog, prince of Rosh, Meshech and Tubal. I will turn you about and put hooks into you jaws, and I will bring you out, and all your army, horses and horsemen, all of them splendidly attired, a great company with buckler and shield, all of them wielding swords; Persia, Ethiopia and Put with them, all of them with shield and helmet. Gomer with all its troops; Beth-togarmah from the remote parts of the north with all it troops— many peoples with you."'"*

Some of these names might seem a little strange, for Ezekiel uses the ancient geographic names that existed in his day. But when we look at the countries that hold these areas today we discover that it reads like a who's who list of Israel's current enemies.

Here are the nine specific geographical locations listed in Ezekiel 38:1–6.

Ancient Names of Modern Nations

Ancient Name	Modern Nation
Rosh (Ancient Sarmatians—known as Rashu, Rasapu, Ros, and Rus)	**Russia**
Magog (Ancient Scythians)	**Central Asia** (Islamic southern republics of the former Soviet Union with a population of 60 million Muslims. This territory could include modern Afghanistan)
Meshech (Ancient Muschki and Musku in Cilicia and Cappadocia)	**Turkey**
Tubal (Ancient Tubalu in Cappadocia)	**Turkey**
Persia (Name changed to Iran in 1935)	**Iran**
Ethiopia (Ancient Cush, south of Egypt)	**Sudan**
Put (west of Egypt)	**Libya**
Gomer (Ancient Cimmerians—from seventh century to the first century B.C. in central/western Anatolia)	**Turkey**
Beth-togarmah (Til-garimmu—between ancient Carchemish and Haran)	**Turkey**

From this list it is clear that at least six key allies will come together for this invasion: Russia, Turkey, Iran, Libya, Sudan, and the nations of Central Asia. The list reads like the headlines of this week's newspaper! Amazingly, all except Russia are Muslim nations. Iran, Libya, and Sudan are three of Israel's most ardent opponents and are listed by the U.S. government as states that support terrorism. Many of these nations are also either forming or strengthening their ties with one another as these words are being written. It's not too difficult to imagine them conspiring together to invade Israel in the near future.

Ezekiel says that these Islamic nations, led by Russia, will come against Israel "in the last days" at a time when the people of Israel are living in peace and prosperity (see Ezekiel 38:8–12). This probably describes the first half of the Tribulation, when Israel will be living under her peace treaty with Antichrist. Near the middle of the Tribulation, Russia and her Islamic allies will descend upon the nation of Israel "like a storm . . . like a cloud covering the land" (38:9).

So far, so good.

BUT WHERE'S BABYLON?

As you read the list of nations that will invade Israel in the end times, one nation is conspicuous by its absence. Turkey is mentioned, along with Iran, the Islamic nations of Central Asia, Russia, Sudan, and Libya. But where is Iraq? Where is Babylon?

If there is one Muslim nation today that would love to invade, plunder, and annihilate Israel, it's Iraq. But I believe Iraq's absence from this invasion is quite clear if we follow God's blueprint for the end times in Scripture.

First, as we have seen, Babylon will be a great commercial capital for the Antichrist. The Antichrist, according to Daniel 9:27, will make a seven-year peace pact with Israel. The signing of this covenant is actually the event that begins the seven-year Tribulation period.

If Antichrist has his commercial, eastern capital in Babylon, then it's not hard to figure out why Iraq will not join the rest of these Muslim nations when they invade Israel just before the middle of the seven-year Tribulation. Babylon will be controlled by Antichrist, the leader of the Western world.

God's destruction of this Islamic coalition, as recorded in Ezekiel 38–39, will pave the way for Antichrist to take control of the world. When he does so, he will solidify his economic capital in Babylon.

Second, the Bible says that Babylon will be destroyed at the end of the Tribulation just before Jesus comes back to earth. According to Ezekiel 38, the Islamic invaders will be destroyed in the first half of the Tribulation. The omission of Babylon from Ezekiel 38 is consistent with God's predictions elsewhere about her destiny. She will not meet her doom with the other Islamic nations just before the middle of the Tribulation, but will be destroyed later. Babylon has her own personal appointment with destiny.

Babylon will meet her doom on the road to Armageddon.

CHAPTER ELEVEN

LAST STOP: BABYLON

Revelation 19:11–21 describes the greatest event in human history, the second coming of Jesus Christ to earth as King of kings and Lord of lords. Every time I read these words, chills run up my spine:

> *And I saw heaven opened, and behold, a white horse, and He who sat on it is called Faithful and True, and in righteousness He judges and wages war. His eyes are a flame of fire, and on His head are many diadems; and He has a name written on Him which no one knows except Himself. He is clothed with a robe dipped in blood, and His name is called The Word of God. And the armies which are in heaven, clothed in fine linen, white and clean, were following Him on white horses. From His mouth comes a sharp sword, so that with it He may strike down the nations, and He will rule them with a rod of iron; and He treads the wine press of the fierce wrath of God, the Almighty.*
>
> *And on His robe and on His thigh He has a name written, "KING OF KINGS, AND LORD OF LORDS." Then I saw an angel standing in the sun, and he cried out with a*

loud voice, saying to all the birds which fly in midheaven, "Come, assemble for the great supper of God, so that you may eat the flesh of kings and the flesh of commanders and the flesh of mighty men and the flesh of horses and of those who sit on them and the flesh of all men, both free men and slaves, and small and great." And I saw the beast and the kings of the earth and their armies assembled to make war against Him who sat on the horse and against His army.

And the beast was seized, and with him the false prophet who performed the signs in his presence, by which he deceived those who had received the mark of the beast and those who worshiped his image; these two were thrown alive into the lake of fire which burns with brimstone. And the rest were killed with the sword which came from the mouth of Him who sat on the horse, and all the birds were filled with their flesh. (Revelation 19:11–21)

Have you ever stopped to ask yourself what the final event on earth will be *before* that great climactic event of the ages, Jesus' return to planet Earth?

It is the utter destruction of Babylon.

Babylon is the last stop in God's prophetic program—His cataclysmic, end-of-our-world train ride—before the glorious coming of Christ to earth.

Let's see what God says about the final destiny of Babylon.

THE RUIN OF RELIGIOUS BABYLON

As has been pointed out several times already, Babylon, from its rebellious beginning, has represented both a city and the religious system associated with that city. It shouldn't surprise us, then, that when the book of Revelation presents Babylon's final destruction, both of these aspects are in view.

I believe that these two aspects of Babylon are destroyed at two different times, by two different forces.

Revelation 17:16–17 indicates that, even as the ten kings of the reunited Roman Empire give all their power and authority to Antichrist, the religious system of Babylon will be destroyed.

> *And the ten horns which you saw, and the beast, these will hate the harlot and will make her desolate and naked, and will eat her flesh and will burn her up with fire. For God has put it in their hearts to execute His purpose by having a common purpose, and by giving their kingdom to the beast, until the words of God will be fulfilled.* (Revelation 17:16–17)

By the middle of the Tribulation, the Antichrist will have no more use for the harlot religious system of Babylon that has emerged after the Rapture. He will tire of her influence and control over him.

When this harlot religious system has worn out her usefulness to Antichrist, she will be destroyed. In her place, Antichrist will substitute his own new religion. Antichrist's religious system will be simple, yet shocking—"Worship me as god or die!"

The final form of Babylonian religion will be its most blatant, egregious, and arrogant. Antichrist will exalt himself as god incarnate and demand worldwide worship (see Revelation 13:4–8, 11–18). What began at the tower of Babel will reach its diabolical zenith during the final three and one-half years of this age.

BABYLON AND THE ROAD TO ARMAGEDDON

Although the religious system of Babylon will be destroyed by Antichrist and his henchmen at the midpoint of the seven-year Tribulation period, the city of Babylon and its great political, commercial center will not be destroyed until the end of the Tribulation, by a military force opposed to Antichrist as part of the final campaign of Armageddon.

The word *Armageddon* has become synonymous with man's worst fear of the end of the world. But many people don't realize that Armageddon is actually a real place in northern Israel, which overlooks a large valley. Napoleon called it the most ideal battlefield he had ever seen.

Armageddon is the place where the armies of the earth will gather for the final assault against Israel. The Bible refers to Armageddon as a "war," or a military campaign that will play out in several stages, not a single battle (Revelation 16:14).

THE FIRST STAGE OF ARMAGEDDON

The first stage of the Campaign of Armageddon is the assembling of the troops of Antichrist and his allies at Armageddon. This begins with the sixth bowl judgment recorded in Revelation 16:12–16:

*The sixth angel poured out his bowl on the great
river, the Euphrates; and its water was dried up,
so that the way would be prepared for the kings
from the east. And I saw coming out of the
mouth of the dragon and out of the mouth of
the beast and out of the mouth of the false
prophet, three unclean spirits like frogs; for they
are spirits of demons, performing signs, which
go out to the kings of the whole world, to gather
them together for the war of the great day of
God, the Almighty. ("Behold, I am coming like
a thief. Blessed is the one who stays awake and
keeps his clothes, so that he will not walk about
naked and men will not see his shame.") And
they gathered them together to the place which
in Hebrew is called Har-Magedon.*

THE SECOND STAGE OF ARMAGEDDON

The second stage of the Campaign of Armageddon is the
destruction of the city of Babylon, as recorded in Revelation
18. When Antichrist begins his drive toward Armageddon in
Israel, some of his enemies, who have chafed under his iron
fist, will seize the opportunity and attack Babylon.

The attack on Babylon by many nations is described in
Jeremiah 50:9–10:

*"For behold, I am going to arouse and bring
up against Babylon a horde of great nations
from the land of the north, and they will*

draw up their battle lines against her; from
there she will be taken captive. Their arrows
will be like an expert warrior who does not
return empty-handed. Chaldea will become
plunder; all who plunder her will have
enough,” declares the LORD.

The sudden, shocking, total destruction of Babylon is also compellingly described in Revelation 18:8, 10: "For this reason in one day her plagues will come, pestilence and mourning and famine, and she will be burned up with fire; for the Lord God who judges her is strong…. 'Woe, woe, the great city, Babylon, the strong city! For in one hour your judgment has come.'"

When the city is destroyed, all the merchants and kings of the earth will mourn for the great city, not because she got what she deserved, but because they will no longer be able to use her to line their own pockets (see Revelation 18:9–11).

The judgment of Babylon will be from God. But he will use human armies to mete out His wrath against the city.

THE FINAL STAGE OF ARMAGEDDON

The final phase of Armageddon is the second coming of Christ to destroy the armies of Antichrist and his allies, as recorded in Revelation 19:15–21.

Babylon will be destroyed once and for all, just as Isaiah and Jeremiah predicted so long ago. She will fall never to rise again.

APOCALYPSE NOW?

During the Gulf War crisis, many people wondered if that was the beginning of Armageddon. Interest in Bible prophecy peaked. Now, world focus is once more on Iraq. The same questions are coming up again. Could this be Armageddon?

Of course, anyone who understands Bible prophecy knows that current events cannot be Armageddon.

I do believe, however, that the showdown in Iraq, while it has nothing to do with Armageddon, does in a sense prefigure or preview what will happen there in the future when Babylon is destroyed by a host of nations. Saddam Hussein once called the Persian Gulf War the "Mother of all Battles," but actually, that phrase better describes Armageddon, which is yet to come.

All the attention on Iraq today is paving the way for Babylon to take its place for one final curtain call before the end of the age.

SINGING THE HALLELUJAH CHORUS

The word *hallelujah,* which means "praise God," occurs only four times in the entire New Testament. And all four occurrences come in Revelation 19:1–6 in response to the destruction of the city of Babylon in Revelation 18:

> *After these things I heard something like a loud voice of a great multitude in heaven, saying, "Hallelujah! Salvation and glory and power belong to our God; BECAUSE HIS JUDGMENTS ARE TRUE AND RIGHTEOUS; for He has judged the great harlot who was corrupting*

the earth with her immorality, and HE HAS AVENGED THE BLOOD OF HIS BOND-SERVANTS ON HER." And a second time they said, "Hallelujah! HER SMOKE RISES UP FOREVER AND EVER." And the twenty-four elders and the four living creatures fell down and worshiped God who sits on the throne saying, "Amen, Hallelujah!" And a voice came from the throne, saying, "Give praise to our God, all you His bond-servants, you who fear Him, the small and the great." Then I heard something like the voice of a great multitude and like the sound of many waters and like the sound of mighty peals of thunder, saying, "Hallelujah! For the Lord our God, the Almighty, reigns." (Revelation 19:1–6)

Revelation 19:1–6 is a fulfillment of the words of Jeremiah 51:48. "'Then heaven and earth and all that is in them will shout for joy over Babylon, for the destroyers will come to her from the north,' declares the LORD."

Imagine the scene. Babylon has just been wiped out on earth by a mighty show of force from the north. She is ruined. She is smoldering in ashes. The sea captains are mourning. The kings of the earth are in shock. The armies of the world are making their way to Armageddon in Israel for the final showdown.

And what is heaven's response to all of this?

"Praise God!"
  "Praise God!"
    "Praise God!"
      "Praise God!"

Not exactly what we would expect. The only time in the New Testament where the "Hallelujah Chorus" is heard is in response to the wrath of God against Babylon. Why is this? Why are heaven and earth so overjoyed to see the end of Babylon?

In these hallelujahs in Revelation 19:1–6, I believe we see at least two key indications of the reason for all the excitement.

First, we read:

> *After these things I heard something like a loud voice of a great multitude in heaven, saying, "Hallelujah! Salvation and glory and power belong to our God; BECAUSE HIS JUDGMENTS ARE TRUE AND RIGHTEOUS; for He has judged the great harlot who was corrupting the earth with her immorality, and HE HAS AVENGED THE BLOOD OF HIS BOND-SERVANTS ON HER." And a second time they said, "Hallelujah! HER SMOKE RISES UP FOREVER AND EVER." And the twenty-four elders and the four living creatures fell down and worshiped God who sits on the throne saying, "Amen. Hallelujah!"* (Revelation 19:1–4)

I believe this means that, by destroying Babylon, God proves that He is righteous and true in judgment. God had foretold centuries earlier, in Isaiah and Jeremiah, that Babylon would fall never to rise again. The final doom of Babylon in Revelation 17–18 is the fulfillment of these ancient prophecies. It proves that God is righteous and true. That He keeps His Word. All heaven rejoices.

On the other hand, if Babylon were not destroyed God would not be righteous and true in His judgment. He would have let Babylon off the hook. That she is destroyed is cause for great rejoicing, because her destruction validates the perfection of the character of almighty God.

Second, the final destruction of Babylon paves the way for the kingdom of Christ to come to earth. Revelation 19:6 says, "Hallelujah! For the Lord our God, the Almighty, reigns." With the destruction of Babylon, the last order of business has been taken care of on earth before Christ can come to set up His glorious kingdom.

This is something to shout about.

"The kingdom of the world has become the kingdom of our Lord and of His Christ; and He will reign forever and ever" (Revelation 11:15).

FULL CIRCLE

One of the amazing things about the book of Revelation is how so many themes and ideas that are introduced in Genesis, the book of beginnings, find their counterpart in this book of culmination. What began in Genesis is brought to completion in Revelation.

Beginnings and Completions	
Genesis	**Revelation**
Heavens and earth created (1:1)	New heavens and earth (21:1)
Sun created (1:16)	No need of the sun (21:23)
Night established (1:5)	No night (22:5)
Seas created (1:10)	No more seas (21:1)
River in the Garden of Eden (2:10–14)	River from the throne of God (22:1)
Death enters history (3:19)	No more death (21:4)
Man driven from Eden (3:24)	Man restored to paradise (22:2, 14)
Sorrow and pain begin (3:17)	No more tears and pain (21:4)

The same is true of Babylon. Babylon is introduced in the Bible in Genesis 10–11 as man's city and ultimately Satan's city. In the end times, Babylon will again become Satan's headquarters for a brief time. Then, religious Babylon will be destroyed near the middle of the Tribulation, and the city and its commercial system will meet its doom at the hands of invaders just before Christ returns to earth.

God will finally destroy Satan's city, New Babylon, and all that it represents, and will establish His city, New Jerusalem, in all its glory.

History will have come full circle.

God's city will prevail.

HOW CLOSE ARE WE?

Before New Babylon can be destroyed, it must be rebuilt. I know what you're thinking. How close are we to seeing this city rise on the international scene? Is it possible that Babylon could be rebuilt soon? Are there any clues that point to its rise?

Even now Babylon is being prepared for its final appearance on the stage of human history. Join me as we scan the horizon for signs that indicate its coming could be very soon.

CHAPTER TWELVE

BABYLON TODAY: SETTING THE STAGE

We have seen an overview of Babylon's past and future in the pages of God's Word. And we have discovered that the prophecies concerning Babylon's final destruction have never been literally fulfilled.

In view of these things, I believe that Babylon must be rebuilt in the end times as a center of commercialism, greed, and pride. She must then suffer total annihilation at the hand of God to literally fulfill what the Bible says.

The late J. Vernon McGee, a well-known Bible teacher with Thru the Bible Radio Network, suggested the following scenario:

> In that day Babylon will dominate and rule the world. The capital of Antichrist will be Babylon, and he will have the first total dictatorship. The world will be an awful place. In that day everything will center in Babylon. The stock market will be read from Babylon—not New York. . . . Everything in the city will be in rebellion against Almighty God, and it centers in Antichrist.[35]

Now we need to ask, "Do the events in Babylon today point toward the fulfillment of the Biblical predictions for that place?" Could ancient Babylon on the Euphrates River actually be rebuilt as a major world economic center? Is this really possible?

I believe we can identify five main factors falling into place at this very moment, indicating that Babylon could quickly become the city described in end-time prophecy.

READY TO REBUILD

First, Saddam Hussein, who fancied himself as a modern Nebuchadnezzar, began restoration and building efforts in ancient Babylon on the Euphrates more than ten years ago. Although the rebuilding efforts are incomplete, the fact that initial steps have already been taken is incredible.

Rick MacInnes-Rae of CBC Radio visited Babylon and described what he saw there in 2002:

> Babylon. The name has given me shivers ever since I read about it as a child. But finally visiting it, one white-hot day in Iraq, had a grisly poignancy I hadn't expected to find. . . . Centuries of pillage and rising water left little of the original buildings. Until Saddam Hussein stepped in. He ordered the complex rebuilt, and it has been, though the work is a little shabby and Babylon's great treasures now lie in foreign museums. But in the background, on a nearby hillside, is another of Saddam's constructions. It's one of his fabled palaces, his personal Babylon; a building so large it might easily hold a crowd of 10,000. . . .

> A plaque on the wall outside Babylon makes
> it clear Saddam sees himself as the
> Nebuchadnezzar of his generation. He proudly
> believes rebuilding Babylon makes him its
> modern-day patron, and a modern-day king.[36]

The first steps in the rebuilding of Babylon are just that—first steps. We can expect that others will take up where Saddam left off in the months and years ahead.

BLACK GOLD

Second, Iraq sits on at least the second largest crude oil reserves in the world. Here is a quick overview of the known oil reserves of the top four oil-rich nations.[37]

Middle East Oil Reserves	
Company	Reserves
Saudi Arabian Oil Company	260 billion barrels
Iraqi National Oil Company	113 billion barrels
National Iranian Oil	100 billion barrels
Kuwait Petroleum Corporation	97 billion barrels

The total estimated proven oil reserves in the world are about 1,000 billion barrels. In terms of proven reserves, this means that Saudi Arabia has about 26 percent, Iraq has 11 percent, and Iran and Kuwait each have about 10 percent. That's about 56 percent for these four nations alone. They are literally floating on a sea of oil.

Incredibly, some believe that Iraq may even have as

many as 300 billion barrels, which would then equal about 25 percent of the known reserves in the world (because the total would then rise to at least 1,200 billion barrels). Oil exploration in Iraq has not been as extensive as that in Saudi Arabia and Kuwait, so we can't be sure. But the reserve life of Iraq's oil at the present rate of production is currently estimated at about 90 years. In other words, no matter how the final numbers play out, Iraq will be a major player in the world oil market, if not *the* major player, for a long time.

If these estimates are accurate, then Iraq, Saudi Arabia, Iran, and Kuwait together could have more than 60 percent of the proven oil reserves in the world. That's staggering.

If Iraq does have 300 billion barrels of the world's oil, and you use the price of $30 per barrel, some have estimated that this equals $500,000 worth of crude oil for every man, woman, and child in the country.

And we must remember who put the oil there.

God did.

It all fits into His blueprint for the end times. It's no accident that Babylon is in Iraq, a nation with such staggering oil reserves. God said that Babylon will be rebuilt as a great commercial center in the end times.

The oil is what is drawing the world back to Babylon. Eighty years ago it seemed totally ludicrous and far-fetched that world power could return to the Middle East. To Iraq. But something incredible happened in 1927 with the discovery of oil there, complemented by the rise of oil-dependent machines and technology. It's not difficult today to see why a world leader like Antichrist would build a capital there. The wealth of the world is moving to that part of the planet.

Ironically, the ouster of Saddam from power actually makes the rebuilding of Babylon much more likely. Saddam's eight-year war with neighboring Iran in the 1980s, and the twelve years of U.N. sanctions in the wake of the Gulf War, have left Iraq financially drained. Also, from 1980 to 2002, Saddam never took full advantage of his massive oil reserves. He did a lot of military building, but his insane ego and legendary impatience left the country in dire financial straits with a deteriorated national infrastructure.

His removal from power will result in a lifting of the sanctions and limitations on Iraqi oil sales. Billions of dollars, euros, and yen will begin to flood into Iraq again to rebuild the infrastructure, improve oil production, and even explore new, unproven oil fields.

All by itself, wealth from Iraq's huge oil reserves makes the rebuilding of Babylon as a major economic center for the Middle East and the world a serious possibility. If Iraq were to successfully annex Kuwait in the future, as they tried to do in 1991, the country could control up to one-third of the world's oil reserves.

What better place for Antichrist to locate a major economic center than Babylon? It's in the geographic center of the Persian Gulf area, surrounded by rich oil reserves. It's not far from Iraq's borders with Iran, Kuwait, and Saudi Arabia, thus affording a strategic location between these four oil-rich nations. What more propitious location for a world economic, commercial center than right in the middle of up to two-thirds of the world's black gold?

THE RISE OF BABYLON

Third, Iraq has become—and continues to be—the major focal point in the Middle East and the Persian Gulf. It's interesting to me that Iraq has seemingly sprung up out of nowhere in the past ten to fifteen years to play a key role on the world's stage.

Iraq did not even become a sovereign nation until 1932, established as part of the British Mandate after World War I. It had a ten-year mandate period beginning in 1922, during which the country was administrated by Britain. At the end of this ten-year period, Iraq achieved its independence.

Again, this is no accident. Sixteen years after Iraq's independence, Israel became a nation in 1948. Nine years later, in 1957, the European Common Market was founded. The Common Market has evolved into the current EU. The rise of Babylon is lining up with other key signs of the times.

Knowing what the Bible says about Babylon in the end times, the meteoric rise of Iraq in recent years shouldn't surprise us. In fact, it is a perfect prelude for the building of Babylon in the near future.

GLORY DAYS

Fourth, Babylon is the ancient capital of King Nebuchadnezzar and the mighty Neo-Babylonian empire. It seems very likely to me that, in a new Iraq, every attempt could be made to give the people a link to their past greatness. Rebuilding the ancient city of Babylon could be one way to rebuild the morale of the Iraqi people. Westerners who will be anxious to cultivate the Iraqi people and their new regime, for any of a variety of reasons, might offer to help rebuild Babylon as a gesture of good will and cultural sensitivity.

Although we don't know exactly how Babylon will be rebuilt or what will motivate men to carry out this task, I believe that the Bible says it will occur. And current events seem to indicate that it could be soon.

IT'S ALL ABOUT POLITICS

Fifth, when the Antichrist comes to power over the EU, it makes sense that he would place his new capital in a neutral location. If the Antichrist were to select a site in one of the nations of the EU, this would undoubtedly be resisted by the other nations. Jealousies would abound.

A site such as Babylon, however, would be a perfect "neutral" location that would help Antichrist keep the peace while he continues his ascent to power.

HOW QUICKLY CAN BABYLON BE REBUILT?

One question I know you are asking is, "How long would it take to build a city of this magnitude in modern Iraq?" It's one thing to say that a city will be built, but is it really feasible?

Some might even suggest that if the rebuilding of Babylon is part of the end-time events, then that means Jesus can't come back for at least twenty years. Obviously, it would take *years* to build a city like this.

Or would it?

To show how quickly a city can rise out of nowhere, consider the story of Oak Ridge, Tennessee. Until 1942, the area where Oak Ridge is located was rural and remote despite being only twenty miles from Knoxville. That all changed dramatically when the government decided to build three facilities there to extract uranium-235 isotopes from uranium ore as part of our country's efforts to build an atom bomb. The Army built a complete city there virtually overnight, with shopping centers, schools, cafeterias, entertainment, a hospital, a newspaper, and other facilities. Within eighteen months the city had 100,000 residents. A huge bus network was quickly developed to provide transportation for the residents around town, to the three plants, and to Knoxville.

Amazingly, we also have a very recent example of a new city in the Middle East rising from the sand dunes. It's called Dubai Internet City. This new city is referred to as an oasis in the desert. Dubai Internet City is being heralded as the most ambitious engineering, business, and political project in the Middle East. The new city, located in the United Arab Emirates, is just a few kilometers from the city of Dubai.

In 2001, Dubai Internet City had ten buildings with three hundred companies and 3,500 users. The site contains lakes, trees, and oases, and occupies over four hundred acres. Currently, more than 350 additional applications from major enterprises for office space are being considered.

During 2002, the city was slated to add fourteen more office buildings and 120 luxury residential villas. Here is the astounding part. *Dubai Internet City was designed, built, and made available to tenants in only twelve months.*

At the opening ceremony for the new community, Sheikh Mohammed bin Rashid Al Maktoum told the audience: "I had a vision to transform the old economy by making Dubai a hub for the new economy. This is a project to be pursued with energy and efficiency…this is Dubai's future."[38] The city was built to serve the entire region, from Morocco to the Indian subcontinent.

Although no one is claiming supercity status for this phenomenon in the dunes, its rise as an economic and technological center in such a brief time shows how quickly a city can rise in the Middle East desert. With incredible oil wealth and the power of Antichrist, Babylon could be rebuilt in a relatively short time.

It could be only a matter of months.

WHERE'S AMERICA?

As I've already stated, Mark Hitchcock is neither a prophet nor the son of a prophet. But I'd be willing to wager you might have one nagging question about this whole scenario.

Where is America in all this?

After all, America is the greatest military, political, economic power the world has ever known. We are miles ahead of our nearest rival. We are the only remaining superpower in the world. However, one thing that has always puzzled students of Bible prophecy is the complete absence of any mention of—or allusion to—America in the Bible. How can we explain this deafening silence concerning America in the end times? The only reasonable explanation is that something dramatic must happen to America.

Otherwise, how could Babylon realistically become the great economic hub of the world, supplanting New York City and the United States? Would it really be possible for

Babylon to rise to such prominence in the shadow of a vast superpower like the U.S.A.?

How could such a thing happen?

Actually, the answer might be quite simple. *The Rapture!*

Think about it. If the Rapture were to happen today, if all the true believers in Jesus Christ were whisked away to heaven in a split second, America would be devastated beyond comprehension. Consider these most recent statistics from Barna Research Online.

Eighty-five percent of Americans claim to be Christians. This group is often identified as cultural Christians.

Forty-one percent of Americans claim to be born-again Christians. This is a subset of the broad Christian group.

Seven percent of American adults are identified as evangelical Christians. This group is a subset of the born-again group. The main factor in this category is a belief that salvation is by faith in Christ alone, without human works. According to Barna, this represents about 14–16 million American adults. Adding in children, the number could easily climb to 25–30 million.[39]

In his book *Operation World,* Patrick Johnstone records the number of evangelical Christians in America as 23 percent of the total population. The total population of America according to the 2000 census is 281,421,906. Using Johnstone's figures, the total number of believers in America is about 65 million.[40]

Even if we use Barna's lower figures, at least 25–30 million Americans are believers in Christ. That—at least—is how many Americans will disappear all at once when the Rapture occurs. And the number could be as high as 65 million. The impact will be nothing short of cataclysmic. Not only would our country lose a minimum of 10 percent of her population, but she would lose the very best, the salt and light of this great land (see Matthew 5:13–14).

The same cannot be legitimately said of any other nation in the world. Patrick Johnstone gives the following statistics for the number of believers in various regions of the world:

United States	23 percent
Asia	2.7 percent
Africa	11.9 percent
Middle East	0.28 percent
Latin America	9.1 percent

And the numbers for Europe are staggering. Johnstone says that, of the forty-three European nations, twenty-two are less than 1 percent evangelical and eleven are less than 0.2 percent. The Rapture will be a blip on the radar screen for many nations and entire regions of the world.

But not so in America.

The immediate ripple effect of the Rapture will touch every area of our society. Millions of mortgages will go unpaid, military personnel by the thousands will be permanently AWOL, factory workers will never show up for work again, college tuition loans will never be repaid, businesses will be left without workers and leaders, the Dow will crash, the NASDAQ will plummet, and the entire economy will be thrown into chaos. Those who are left behind in America will be left behind to pick up the pieces.

It's very likely that America will be brought to her knees by the Rapture. The Rapture is the key. The Rapture will change everything. There's an old saying that nature abhors a vacuum. I believe the Rapture will produce a vacuum of power that the Antichrist and his reunited Roman Empire will step in to fill in the end times. And Babylon will rise as the city pictured in God's Word to take her place at center stage.

EYE ON IRAQ

Is the rise of Iraq to world prominence an accident? Is the incredible oil wealth of Iraq just a stroke of good fortune? I don't think so. The resurgence of Iraq, the efforts that have already been made to restore and rebuild Babylon, and the incredible oil wealth available to finish rebuilding the city all point toward the picture the Bible paints for Babylon in the end times.

Charles Dyer notes the significance of the rise of Iraq:

> Babylon is pictured as a place that sea captains and merchants are going to. It's a place that controls the world economically with her wealth, that even somehow has a relationship to the Antichrist. The Antichrist is military power, but this economic power exerts control over him.
>
> God put the oil in the ground, God sets the stage of world history, and I believe when the final events are ready, when the final curtain goes up, Babylon's going to be there. It's going to be there as an economic powerhouse. It's not there yet. Saddam Hussein has not made Babylon all that the Bible says it

will be, but Saddam Hussein or someone who follows him could make it that in a matter of weeks. All it would take is controlling the oil wealth and then saying, 'I'm going to make that place even greater than I've made it so far. It's going to become my capital.' And at that point, Babylon is everything the Bible says it would be.[41]

Keep your eye on Iraq in the days ahead. Current events there are another part of the matrix of events in the Middle East that are setting the stage for the coming Middle East crisis predicted in God's Word.

CHAPTER THIRTEEN

HOW TO BE RAPTURE READY!

On one occasion when He was with the religious leaders of His day, Jesus made a very important statement we need to keep in mind. In Matthew 16:1–3, Jesus sternly rebuked the religious leaders of His day for their blindness to the signs of the times of His first coming.

> *The Pharisees and Sadducees came up, and testing Jesus, they asked Him to show them a sign from heaven. But he replied to them, "When it is evening, you say, 'It will be fair weather, for the sky is red.' And in the morning, 'There will be a storm today, for the sky is red and threatening.' Do you know how to discern the appearance of the sky, but cannot discern the signs of the times?"*

Jesus had burst on the scene performing the prophesied miracles of the Messiah right before their eyes, and yet they were blind to the clear signs of His first coming.

Likewise today, many are following the same sad pattern. They are blind to the things that are happening in the world—events related to God's program for the second coming of Christ.

DARK SHADOWS

I try to jog at least three times a week, so I can eat more. Not long ago I was going out to jog a couple of miles. I started off by walking for a few minutes to get warmed up. As I walked along the sidewalk I happened to noticed something I don't notice every day.

It was my shadow, cast on the concrete before me.

My shadow is not me. It's not the substance of me. In some ways it resembles me, but in many others ways, not at all.

Yet it is a sign.

When you see Mark Hitchcock's shadow, you can count on the fact that Mark Hitchcock is near at hand. It's a sign that I am coming. (Not very quickly, perhaps, but with great certainty!)

In the same way, coming events often cast their shadows upon this world before they arrive, functioning as what we know as "signs of the times."

It is happening right now as you read these words. Future events are casting their shadows before us. As we have seen, there are five primary discernible shadows on the ground right now.

1. Israel, after 1,900 years of exile, is being regathered to her ancient homeland. *It's a shadow of what is coming.*

2. The Roman Empire, 1,600 years after being broken apart, is being reunited before our eyes in the European Union. More nations are petitioning for entrance. The stage is set for one man to come on the scene to take

over the EU and fulfill the Bible's prophecies of a final world ruler over the reunited Roman Empire. *It's a shadow of what will be.*

3. Militant Muslims would love nothing more than to pour into Israel to plunder her as the Bible predicts in Ezekiel 38–39. *It's a shadow of great events just ahead.*

4. The world yearns for someone to bring peace to the Israeli-Palestinian problem. Peace in the Middle East is international priority number one. According to Daniel 9:27, Antichrist bursts on the world stage by forging a peace agreement with Israel (see Revelation 6:1–2). *It's a shadow of vast changes already on their way.*

5. Events in Iraq make the rise of New Babylon, predicted in Scripture, seem more likely every day. Iraq has only been a modern nation since 1932. Oil wasn't discovered there until 1927. Yet this nation is already front and center in the world. Current geopolitical conditions, in conjunction with the rich oil reserves surrounding Babylon, make it a perfect setting for Antichrist's economic capital. *It's a shadow right in front of us—with the reality already bearing down.*

With these signs converging before our eyes, we ought to be asking how we should respond. How we can make sure we're ready for the Rapture?

PARDON ME!

No person knows how much time he has left on this earth, either personally or prophetically. Personally, all of us are painfully aware of our mortality. None of us have any guarantee of seeing tomorrow.

Prophetically, Christ could come at any moment to take His bride, the church, to heaven, and all unbelievers would be left behind to endure the horrors of the Tribulation period.

With this in mind, the most important question for every reader to face is whether he or she has a personal relationship with Jesus Christ.

If you have never personally accepted Jesus Christ as your Savior from sin, then you need to accept Him right now. The only way to come into a relationship with God and gain admission to heaven is through God's Son, Jesus Christ.

You see, we all have a terrible problem. There's a barrier that keeps us away from God. There's a barrier that keeps us from having a relationship with God. And that barrier is our sins. The Bible declares that God is infinitely holy, righteous, and just. He cannot accept sinners into His holy presence. As you can see right off, this is a major problem for us. Because God's Word also tells us that all men and women, including you and me, are sinners both by nature and by action. Romans 3:23 states the problem with sobering clarity: "For all have sinned and fall short of the glory of God."

It's soberingly simple. God is perfect. His glory is perfect. But we all fall short.

Imagine if there were a contest to see who could jump from New York City to London. Most of us lesser mortals could only jump five, ten, or fifteen feet, if that far. Some great jumpers might jump twenty-seven feet. But the problem is that no one would even get close to London. We would all fall short. Far short.

The same thing is true of each of us in our attempts to live up to the standard of God's glorious perfection by our own efforts, our own merit.

So how can a holy God accept sinful man? How can we possibly even come into the presence of the holy God in our sinful condition?

In His infinite wisdom and grace, God long ago formulated a plan to remedy this problem. God the Son agreed to step out of eternity into time, to take on human flesh, to live the sinless life we could never live, and to die in our place. He took all our sins and took all the punishment we deserved. The full wrath of the Father, which should have been poured out on us, was instead heaped upon Jesus when he hung on the cross.

Just before He died, Jesus cried out, "It is finished." The debt for your sins and mine was paid in full. Jesus paid it all. Then, three days later He rose again to prove that the payment had been accepted. The resurrection of Christ from the dead is our receipt that payment in full has been made and accepted. Now all that remains for us is to accept the full pardon for ourselves.

In the year 1829, a Philadelphia man named George Wilson robbed the Reading mail coach, killing someone in the process. Wilson was arrested, brought to trial, found guilty, and sentenced to be hanged. Some friends intervened on his behalf and were finally able to obtain a pardon for him from President Andrew Jackson. But, when he was informed of this, George Wilson refused to accept the pardon!

The sheriff was unwilling to carry out the sentence—how could he hang a pardoned man? An appeal was sent to President Jackson. The perplexed President turned to the United States Supreme Court to decide the case. Chief Justice Marshall ruled that a pardon is a piece of paper, the value of which depends on its acceptance by the person implicated. It is hardly to be expected that a person under the sentence of death would refuse to accept a pardon, but if it is refused it is then not a pardon. It was decided that George Wilson must be hung.

So George Wilson was escorted to the gallows and executed, while his pardon lay on the sheriff's desk.[42]

Not long ago I told this story to a group of young people. After the service, one of the young men came up to me and said, "Why in the world would someone be so stupid and refuse to accept a pardon?"

That's a good question, isn't it. But maybe you are doing the very same thing George Wilson did. You have rejected the pardon God offers you.

The pardon has been purchased by the precious blood of Christ. It is available for you to accept by faith right now, whoever and wherever you are. You don't deserve it. George Wilson didn't deserve Andrew Jackson's pardon either. But it's yours for the taking.

You might ask, "How do I receive it? How do I accept the pardon?" The Bible says you receive it by simply calling on the Lord in prayer. Romans 10:13 says, "For whoever will call upon the name of the Lord will be saved." It is the greatest decision you will ever make. When you receive Christ personally, you will immediately receive forgiveness for all your sins. For the very first time in your life you will enter into a relationship with the living God.

Now that you know some of what is coming upon this world in the last days and how many of these signs seem to be lining up on the horizon, respond to God's gracious invitation before it's too late. Why not call upon the Lord right now to receive His gracious pardon by praying a simple prayer like this?

> "Father, I come to You now and admit that I'm a sinner. And I know that I need a Savior. I acknowledge that I can never earn my own way to heaven. I accept Jesus as the Savior I need. I believe that He died and rose again for me. I receive the full pardon that He purchased for me on the cross. Thank You for saving me and allowing me to know You personally. Amen."

HOW SHOULD WE THEN LIVE?

If you have already received God's free pardon, then knowing what's ahead should have a powerful impact on your daily life as well. Bible prophecy was never given just to spark our imagination or fill our heads with timelines of end-time events. Bible prophecy was intended to transform our lives as we live each day for our Master.

Every passage of Scripture that I can think of that mentions the coming of Jesus Christ contains a clear, practical application for our daily lives.

Here are four of the main effects that I pray your understanding of the end times will produce.

KNOWING WHAT'S AHEAD PROMOTES EVANGELISM

If you are already a believer in Jesus Christ, it's difficult to see what's ahead for this world without being gripped by the awesome power and wrath of God. Understanding Bible prophecy brings us face-to-face with what is at stake for those who don't know Christ as their Savior. We are reminded in 2 Corinthians 5:20 of our calling during this present age. "We are Christ's ambassadors, and God is using us to speak to you. We urge you, as though Christ himself were here pleading with you, 'Be reconciled to God!'"(NLT).

Those who have already responded to the message of God's grace and forgiveness through Christ know where this world is headed, and we are Christ's ambassadors representing Him and His interests to a perishing world.

KNOWING WHAT'S AHEAD PROMOTES PERSONAL PURITY

The Word of God is clear that a proper understanding of Bible prophecy should produce a life of holiness and purity.

> *Yes, dear friends, we are already God's children, and we can't even imagine what we will be like when Christ returns. But we do know that when he comes we will be like him, for we will see him as he really is. And all who believe this will keep themselves pure, just as Christ is pure.*
> (1 John 3:2–3, NLT)

Focusing your heart on the coming of Christ is a fail-safe formula for maintaining personal purity. Note the certainty in that verse: *"And all who believe this will keep themselves pure."*

Here is a perfect prescription for living a life of holiness: focusing on the coming of Christ. Let its reality grip your thoughts, your soul. It's one thing for us to hold right doctrine about Christ's coming. It is another thing for the doctrine to hold us!

In 1988, a book was published entitled *88 Reasons Why Christ Will Return in 1988*. In the book, the author stated that he had conclusive proof that Christ would rapture the Church to heaven in October 1988. A friend of mine who was a pastor in Eastern Oklahoma called me in the summer of 1988 to ask me some questions about the book.

In our conversation he told me that the book had caused quite a furor among many people in his church and other churches in the area. Of course, the Bible clearly declares that date setting concerning the coming of Christ is futile and foolish (see Matthew 24:36; Luke 21:8). This erroneous book, however, caused many people to re-examine their lives—just in case the book was right!

Obviously, the book was totally incorrect, but when people began to consider the fact that Christ might return soon, it transformed their lives. The Bible declares that we are to always be looking for Christ's coming, not just when someone sets an arbitrary date.

> *We should live in this evil world with self-control, right conduct, and devotion to God, while we look forward to that wonderful event when the glory of our great God and Savior, Jesus Christ, will be revealed.* (Titus 2:12–13, NLT)

The practical, cleansing effect of prophecy is also presented in 2 Peter 3:10–14 (NLT):

But the day of the Lord will come as unexpectedly as a thief. Then the heavens will pass away with a terrible noise, and everything in them will disappear in fire, and the earth and everything on it will be exposed to judgment. Since everything around us is going to melt away, what holy, godly lives you should be living! You should look forward to that day and hurry it along—the day when God will set the heavens on fire and the elements will melt away in the flames. But we are looking forward to the new heavens and new earth he has promised, a world where everyone is right with God. And so, dear friends, while you are waiting for these things to happen, make every effort to live a pure and blameless life. And be at peace with God.

KNOWING WHAT'S AHEAD PRODUCES HOPE IN A DARK WORLD

Not long ago I went to eat lunch at a local restaurant. While I was waiting to be served, I noticed that the large TV in the room was tuned to ESPN Classic. After a few minutes, I actually recognized the game being replayed. It was the 1986 AFC Championship game between the Denver Broncos and the Cleveland Browns. What a contest! It truly was a classic gridiron battle.

With 5:32 left in the fourth quarter, the Broncos trailed by a touchdown. And they had the ball on their own two-yard line. They were ninety-eight yards from pay dirt. It was their last shot. Their final chance.

In what now has become known simply as "the drive," John Elway methodically drove his team down the field into scoring position. As I watched the game intently, I found myself getting nervous and anxious. I was for the Broncos.

Then, the obvious came to me. I paused for a moment and thought to myself. *Why am I anxious? I already know who wins. Elway will drive them in for the score. They go into overtime and the Broncos will win with a field goal, 23-20.*

The same is true in our lives. There is much we don't know about this world. We certainly don't know every detail about the end times. There is much we can't know right now.

But when we understand Bible prophecy, we do know one thing for sure.

We know who wins.

The final result is already set. Knowing what's ahead gives us hope, comfort, and confidence in a troubled, uncertain world.

Jesus is coming again for His children, to deliver us from the wrath of the Tribulation period (see 1 Thessalonians 1:9–10). When you face the difficulties, discouragement, and even despair of this life, never forget this fact. If you know Jesus Christ, you will win in Him. There's no reason to be uncertain about the final score.

In John 14:1–4, Jesus said, "Don't be troubled. You trust God, now trust in me. There are many rooms in my Father's home, and I am going to prepare a place for you. If this were not so, I would tell you plainly. When everything is ready, I will come and get you, so that you will always be with me where I am. And you know where I am going and how to get there (NLT)."

The word *troubled* means "to be stirred up, disturbed,

unsettled or thrown into confusion." There are many things in our world today to disturb and unsettle us: the moral decay in our society, crime, economic uncertainty, terrorism, racial unrest, and so on. Added to these problems are the personal trials and difficulties we all face in our daily lives. Trouble is the common denominator of all mankind. Often these troubles and difficulties can leave us distraught, distracted, and disturbed.

On the other hand, knowing what's ahead has a calming influence on us when our hearts get troubled and stirred up. One of the great comforts in times like these is to remember that our Lord will someday return to take us to be with Himself.

In John 14:1–3, our Lord emphasizes three key truths to calm our troubled hearts. These truths encompass a person, a place, and a promise. The person is our Lord, the place is the heavenly city (New Jerusalem), and the promise is that He will come again to take us to be with Him forever.

In other words, no matter how troubled we are, no matter how dark this world looks, we can know one thing beyond all doubt.

We win.

We win because we have a Savior who came to die in our place, rose again, and promised to come again to take us to be with Him forever.

KNOWING WHAT'S AHEAD PROVOKES SACRIFICIAL SERVICE

In 1 Corinthians 15:58, after presenting the truth of the coming of Christ for his people, Paul concludes with a strong admonition. "So, my dear brothers and sisters, be strong and steady, always enthusiastic about the Lord's work, for you know that nothing you do for the Lord is ever useless (NLT)." Paul is saying, "Since you know that Christ will someday come to receive you to Himself, let nothing move you, be strong and steady in your Christian service."

So many today are unstable and unsettled in Christian work. They are constantly vacillating. But knowing about Christ's coming, and knowing something about future events, should cure the problem of instability and inconsistency in our work for the Lord Jesus. Realizing that Christ could return *at any moment* should make us enthusiastic, energetic, and excited about serving the Lord. The first two questions Saul, who later became Paul, asked when he saw the glorified Christ on the road to Damascus were "Who are You, Lord?" and "What shall I do?" (Acts 22:8, 10).

Many professing Christians today have never been past the first question. Many believers in Christ are spiritually unemployed!

Martin Luther, the great reformer, once said that he only had two days on his calendar: "today" and "that day." He said that he always tried to live each day in view of "that day," the day of Christ's coming. This attitude caused him to be a tireless worker for the Lord. Here is a brief overview of what he accomplished in just three years of his life:

1528 (healthy, although one of his daughters died)	**190 sermons and lectures, 150 letters, 20 tracts, work on the Old Testament, and several trips**
1530 (sick for ten months)	**60 sermons and lectures, 170 letters, 30 tracts, work on the Old Testament**
1531 (sick for six months, mother died)	**180 sermons and lectures, 100 letters, 15 tracts, work on the Old Testament, and brief trips.**

The principle in the Bible is clear: waiters are workers. When Christ comes we are to "Be dressed for service and well prepared" (Luke 12:35, NLT). If the events of Bible prophecy are a reality to us, they will motivate us to work faithfully and tirelessly for our Lord until He comes for us.

The Lord intends for our knowledge of Bible prophecy to translate into devoted service for those around us as we await His return.

THE WELCOMING COMMITTEE

Warren Wiersbe tells a story of when he was a young man preaching on the last days with all the events of prophecy clearly laid out and perfectly planned. At the end of the service an older gentleman came up to him and whispered in his ear, "I used to have the Lord's return planned out to the last detail, but years ago I moved from the planning committee to the welcoming committee."

Certainly we want to study Bible prophecy and know about God's plan for the future. That's what this book is all about. That's why I wrote it. But we must be careful not to get so caught up in the planning that we forget the welcoming.

Are you on the welcoming committee for the Lord's return? Are you living each day to please the Master?

May God help us use our knowledge of the end times to transform our lives as we wait for our Savior to return.

It could be today!

A PROPOSED CHRONOLOGY OF THE END TIMES

Any study of Bible prophecy ought to come with the warning, "Some Assembly Required." It's not easy trying to fit together all the pieces of the end times into a chronological sequence. This outline is my best attempt, at this time, to put the pieces together. I certainly wouldn't insist on the correctness of every detail in this outline, but my prayer is that it will help you get a better grasp of the overall flow of events in the end times.

I. EVENTS IN HEAVEN

    A. *The Rapture of the Church* (see 1 Corinthians 15:51–58; 1 Thessalonians 4:13–18; Revelation 3:10)

    B. *The Judgment Seat of Christ* (see Romans 14:10; 1 Corinthians 3:9–15; 4:1–5; 9:24–27; 2 Corinthians 5:10)

    C. *The Marriage of the Lamb* (see 2 Corinthians 11:2; Revelation 19:6–8)

    D. *The Singing of Two Special Songs* (see Revelation 4–5)

    E. *The Lamb Receiving the Seven-Sealed Scroll* (see Revelation 5)

II. EVENTS ON EARTH

A. *Seven-Year Tribulation*

  1. Beginning of the Tribulation

    a. Seven-year Tribulation begins when the Antichrist signs a covenant with Israel, bringing peace to Israel and Jerusalem (see Daniel 9:27; Ezekiel 38:8, 11).

    b. The Jewish temple in Jerusalem is rebuilt (see Daniel 9:27; Revelation 11:1).

    c. The reunited Roman Empire emerges in a ten-nation confederation (see Daniel 2:40–44; 7:7; Revelation 17:12).

  2. First Half (Three and a Half Years) of the Tribulation

    a. The seven seal judgments are opened (see Revelation 6).

    b. The 144,000 Jewish believers begin their great evangelistic ministry (see Revelation 7).

  3. The Midpoint of the Tribulation

    a. Gog and his allies invade Israel and are decimated by God (see Daniel 11:40–45; Ezekiel 38–39).

    b. Antichrist breaks his covenant with Israel and invades the Land (see Daniel 9:27; 11:40–41).

    c. Antichrist begins to consolidate his empire by plundering Egypt, Sudan, and Libya, whose armies have just been destroyed by God in Israel (see Daniel 11:42–43; Ezekiel 38–39).

    d. While in North Africa, Antichrist hears disturbing news of insurrection in Israel and immediately returns there to destroy and annihilate many (see Daniel 11:44).

    e. Antichrist sets up the abomination of desolation in the rebuilt temple in Jerusalem (see Daniel 9:27; 11:45a; Matthew 24:15; 2 Thessalonians 2:4; Revelation 13:5, 15–18).

f. Sometime during these events, the Antichrist is violently killed, possibly as a result of a war or assassination (see Daniel 11:45; Revelation 13:3, 12, 14; 17:8).

g. Satan is cast down from heaven and begins to make war with Israel (see Revelation 12:7–13). The chief means he uses to persecute Israel is the two beasts in Revelation 13.

h. The faithful Jewish remnant flee to Petra in modern Jordan, where they are divinely protected for the remainder of the Tribulation (see Matthew 24:16–20; Revelation 12:15–17).

i. The Antichrist is miraculously raised from the dead to the awestruck amazement of the entire world (see Revelation 13:3).

j. After his resurrection from the dead, the Antichrist gains political control over the ten kings of the reunited Roman Empire. Three of these kings will be killed by the Antichrist, and the other seven will submit (see Daniel 7:24; Revelation 17:12–13).

k. The Two Witnesses begin their three-and-a-half-year ministry (see Revelation 11:3–6).

l. Antichrist and the ten kings destroy the religious system of Babylon and set up their religious capital in the city (see Revelation 17:16–17).

4. Last Half (Three and a Half Years) of the Tribulation

a. Antichrist blasphemes God and the false prophet performs great signs and wonders and promotes false worship of the Antichrist (see Revelation 13:5, 11–15).

    b. The mark of the beast (666) is introduced and enforced by the false prophet (see Revelation 13:16–18).

    c. Totally energized by Satan, the Antichrist dominates the world politically, religiously, and economically (see Revelation 13:4–5, 15–18).

    d. The trumpet judgments are unleashed throughout the final half of the Tribulation (see Revelation 8–9).

    e. Knowing he has only a short time left, Satan intensifies his relentless, merciless persecution of the Jewish people and Gentile believers on earth (see Daniel 7:25; Revelation 12:12; 13:15; 20:4).

5. The End of the Tribulation

    a. The bowl judgments are poured out in rapid succession (see Revelation 16).

    b. The Campaign of Armageddon begins (see Revelation 16:16).

    c. Commercial Babylon is destroyed (see Revelation 18).

    d. The two witnesses are killed by Antichrist and are resurrected by God three and a half days later (see Revelation 11:7–12).

    e. Christ returns to the Mount of Olives and slays the armies gathered against Him throughout the land, from Megiddo to Petra (see Revelation 19:11–16; Isaiah 34:1–6; 63:1–6).

    f. The birds gather to feed on the carnage (see Revelation 19:17–18).

B. *After the Tribulation*

1. Interval or Transition Period of Seventy-Five Days (see Daniel 12:12)

    a. The Antichrist and the false prophet are cast in the lake of fire (see Revelation 19:20–21).

    b. The abomination of desolation is removed from the temple (see Daniel 12:11).

    c. Israel is regathered (see Matthew 24:31).

    d. Israel is judged (see Ezekiel 20:30–39; Matthew 25:1–30).

    e. Gentiles are judged (see Matthew 25:31–46).

    f. Satan is bound in the abyss (see Revelation 20:1–3).

    g. Old Testament and Tribulation saints are resurrected (see Daniel 12:1–3; Isaiah 26:19; Revelation 20:4).

2. One-Thousand-Year Reign of Christ on Earth (see Revelation 20:4–6)

3. Satan's Final Revolt and Defeat (see Revelation 20:7–10)

4. The Great White Throne Judgment of the Lost (see Revelation 20:11–15)

5. The Destruction of the Present Heavens and Earth (see Matthew 24:35; 2 Peter 3:3–12; Revelation 21:1)

6. The Creation of the New Heavens and New Earth (see Isaiah 65:17; 66:22; 2 Peter 3:13; Revelation 21:1)

7. Eternity (see Revelation 21:9–22:5)

Multnomah Publishers®

The publisher and author would love to hear your comments about this book. *Please contact us at:*
www.multnomah.net/hitchcock

NOTES

1. Nancy Gibbs, "The Bible and the Apocalypse," *TIME,* 1 July 2002, 41.

2. Ibid., 40–48.

3. J. A. Seiss, *The Apocalypse: Lectures on the Book of Revelation* (Reprint, Grand Rapids, Mich.: Zondervan Publishing House, 1964), 397.

4. G. H. Pember, *Mystery Babylon the Great and the Mysteries of Catholicism: An Exposition of Revelation,* ed. G. H. Lang (Reprint, Miami Springs, Fla.: Schoettle Publishing Co., 1988), 17–18.

5. Clarence Larkin, *The Book of Revelation* (Glenside, Pa.: Rev. Clarence Larkin Estate, 1919), 150.

6. Arthur W. Pink, *The Antichrist* (1923; reprint, Grand Rapids, Mich: Kregel Publications, 1988), 237–38.

7. F. E. Marsh, "Will Babylon Be Rebuilt," *Associates for Scriptural Knowledge,* 30 September 2002. http://askelm.com/prophecy/p021002.htm (accessed 14 January 2003).

8. William R. Newell, *The Book of Revelation* (Reprint, Chicago: Moody Press, 1981), 268, 272.

9. John F. Walvoord, "Revelation" in *Bible Knowledge Commentary,* ed. John F. Walvoord and Roy B. Zuck (Wheaton, Ill: Victor Books, 1993), 2:970–71.

10. Henry M. Morris, *The Revelation Record* (Wheaton, Ill: Tyndale House, 1983), 329.

11. Donald K. Campbell, *Daniel: God's Man in a Secular Society* (Grand Rapids, Mich.: Discovery House Publishers, 1988), 84.

12. Old Testament references to the Day of the Lord: Isaiah 2:12; 13:6, 9; Ezekiel 13:5; 30:3; Joel 1:15; 2:1, 11, 31; 3:14; Amos 5:18 (2 times); 5:20; Obadiah 15; Zephaniah 1:7, 14 (2 times); Zechariah 14:1; Malachi 4:5. New Testament references: Acts 2:20; 1 Thessalonians 5:2; 2 Thessalonians 2:2; 2 Peter 3:10.

13. Some have suggested that Isaiah 13–14 predicts the destruction of Babylon by Assyria's King Sennacherib that occurred in December 689 B.C. It is true that Babylon was destroyed at that time. But I believe there are four serious problems with correlating Isaiah 13–14 with this destruction. *First,* there is no evidence of cosmic disturbances in 689 B.C. like those described in Isaiah 13:10. *Second,* the judgment on Babylon in 689 was not a worldwide judgment as depicted in Isaiah 13:11–12. *Third,* Babylon's destruction is simultaneous with Israel and Judah's restoration in Isaiah 14. This did not happen in 689 B.C. *Fourth,* the same language for Babylon's total destruction is used in Jeremiah 50:39–40 as is found in Isaiah 13. But we must remember that Jeremiah wrote in about 600 B.C., long after the destruction in 689. It appears that both Jeremiah and Isaiah are describing the same destruction of Babylon not in 689 B.C., but in the end times when Babylon is destroyed once and forever, never to be inhabited again. So one might ask the question, "Does Isaiah

have anything to say about the destruction of Babylon that occurred not long after he wrote?" I believe the answer is yes. It's interesting to note that Babylon's destruction is recorded by Isaiah again in 21:1–10. Why would he give another portrayal of Babylon's judgment after already spending two chapters on it earlier (see Isaiah 13–14)? I believe that Isaiah 13–14 describes the final, eschatological, end-time destruction of Babylon. However, it seems that Isaiah 21:1–10 describes the near destruction of Babylon in December 689 B.C. at the hands of the Assyrians.

14. John F. Walvoord, *The Nations in Prophecy* (Grand Rapids, Mich.: Zondervan Publishing House, 1967), 63–64.

15. Larkin, *The Book of Revelation,* 58.

16. There are four reasons for identifying "he who now restrains," or the restrainer, as the restraining ministry of the Holy Spirit through the church. (1) This restraint requires omnipotent power. The only one with the power to restrain and hold back the appearance of Antichrist is God. (2) This is the only view that adequately explains the change in gender in 2 Thessalonians 2:6–7. The restrainer is both a power—"what restrains him now," and a person—"he who now restrains." In Greek the word *pneuma* (Spirit) is neuter. But the Holy Spirit is also consistently referred to by the masculine pronoun *He,* especially in John 14–16. (3) The Holy Spirit is spoken of in Scripture as restraining sin and evil in the world (see Genesis 6:3) and in the heart of the

believer (see Galatians 5:16–17). (4) The church and its mission of proclaiming and portraying the gospel is the primary instrument the Holy Spirit uses in this age to restrain evil. We are the salt of the earth and the light of the world (see Matthew 5:13–16). We are the temple of the Holy Spirit both individually and corporately.

17. Merrill F. Unger, *Zechariah: Prophet of Messiah's Glory* (Grand Rapids, Mich.: Zondervan Publishing House, 1963), 98; Morris, *The Revelation Record,* 355.

18. Morris, *The Revelation Record,* 355.

19. Ibid., 323.

20. Charles Dyer, *The Rise of Babylon* (Wheaton, Ill.: Tyndale House Publishers, 1991), 182.

21. Morris, *The Revelation Record,* 348–49.

22. Charles H. Dyer, "The Identity of Babylon in Revelation 17–18," *Bibliotheca Sacra* 144 (October–December 1987): 441–43.

23. Arnold Fruchtenbaum, *The Footsteps of the Messiah* (Tustin, Calif.: Ariel Ministries Press, 1983), 161.

24. Robert L. Thomas, *Revelation 8–22* (Chicago: Moody Press, 1995), 282–83

25. John F. Walvoord, *Revelation* (Chicago: Moody Press, 1966), 970.

26. Tim LaHaye and Jerry B. Jenkins, *Left Behind* (Wheaton, Ill.: Tyndale House Publishers, Inc., 1995), 352.

27. Thomas, *Revelation 8–22,* 286.

28. Brandon Mitchener, "A New EU, but No Operating Manual," *The Wall Street Journal,* 16 December 2002.

29. Ibid.

30. "Europe Wakes Up to New Year and New Currency" *CNN.com,* 1 January 1999. http://www.cnn.com/WORLD/europe/9812/31/euro .01/ (accessed 14 January 2003).

31. H. L. Willmington, *The King is Coming* (Wheaton, Ill.: Tyndale House Publishers, 1973), 197.

32. *Webster's New Collegiate Dictionary* (Springfield, Mass.: G. & C. Merriam Company, 1973), 81.

33. Bernard McGinn, *Antichrist: Two Thousand Years of the Human Fascination with Evil* (San Francisco: HarperCollins, 1994), 102.

34. Larkin, *The Book of Revelation,* 161.

35. J. Vernon McGee, *Thru the Bible* (Nashville: Thomas Nelson Publishers, 1983), 5:1039.

36. Rick MacInnes-Rae, "Saddam's Babylon" *CBC News,* August 2002. http://cbc.ca/news/features/iraq/correspondents/ macinnesrae.html (accessed 14 January 2003).

37. Marilyn Radler and Jeanne Stell, *Oil and Gas Journal,* (9 September 2002): 84.

38. Jack Lyne, "Siemens Plugs Regional Telecom HQ into Dubai Internet City," *SiteNet.* http://www.conway.com/ssinsider/bbdeal/bd020408. htm (accessed 14 January 2003).

39. Barna Research Online, "American Faith is Diverse, as Shown among Five Faith-Based Segments," 29 January 2002. http://www.barna.org/cgi-bin/PagePressRelease.asp? PressReleaseID=105&Reference=B (accessed 14 January 2003).

40. Patrick Johnstone, *Operation World* (Grand Rapids, Mich.: Zondervan, 1987), 34.

41. Charles Dyer, "Babylon: Iraq and the Coming Middle East Crisis," in *The Road to Armageddon* (Nashville: Word Publishing, 1999), 136–37.

42. Michael P. Green, ed., *Illustrations for Biblical Preaching* (Grand Rapids: Baker Book House, 1989), 317–18.

HITCHCOCK EXAMINES BIBLE PROPHECY'S SILENCE ABOUT AMERICA

In *Is America in Bible Prophecy*, expert Mark Hitchcock deals with often-raised questions about America's future. Examining three prophetic passages that are commonly thought to describe America, Hitchcock concludes that the Bible is actually silent about the role of the United States in the end times. He then discusses the implications of America's absence in prophetic writings. Along with Hitchcock's compelling forecast for the future, he offers specific actions Americans can take to keep their nation strong and blessed by God as well as an appendix of additional questions and answers.

ISBN 1-57673-496-X

WHAT'S YOUR BIGGEST WORRY ABOUT THE END TIMES?

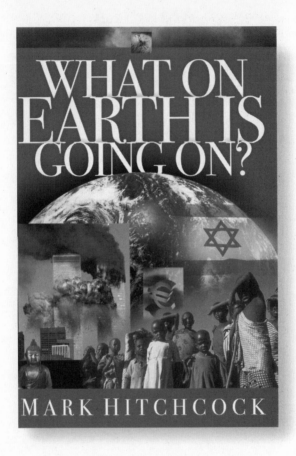

As sensationalists and skeptics wreak havoc with the country's emotions, prophecy expert Mark Hitchcock provides a much-needed definition of "signs of the times." In *What on Earth Is Going On*, Hitchcock discusses the current interest in prophecy caused by the 9/11 attack, presents Jesus' own forecast for the future of the world, and details five major global developments today that discernibly signal Christ's coming. This balanced, concise overview of the real signs of the times will clarify Christ's instructions challenging His followers to be alert in the final days. Readers will easily find and absorb the information they need to prepare for His return.

ISBN 1-57673-853-1

GET READY FOR THE INVASION...

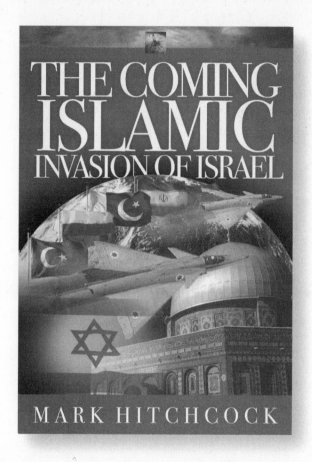

Writing twenty-five hundred years ago, the prophet Ezekiel predicted a Russian-Islamic invasion of Israel in the last days. The third book in Mark Hitchcock's fascinating prophecy series establishes how the current global scene sets the stage for this event, focusing on the identity of the invading nations (those mentioned in Ezekiel are like a *Who's Who* of Israel's current enemies). Hitchcock then considers the timing and motivations for their attack. Finally, he discusses God's dramatic intervention that will pave the way for the Antichrist's worldwide empire.

ISBN 1-59052-048-3

HAS THE STAGE BEEN SET FOR HIS COMING?

Find out what Mark Hitchcock means when he says there is an Antichrist alive today, right now, in this generation! Easy to read and biblically solid, Hitchcock's fascinating resource illuminates what the Bible says about the Antichrist and explains how the prophecies about him strikingly foreshadow today's events such as: the rise of the European Union; the peace process in Israel; the rush toward globalization; the technology and desire for a worldwide identification system; and the movement to rebuild the temple in Jerusalem.

ISBN 1-59052-075-0

HOW WILL WE KNOW
THE END IS NEAR?

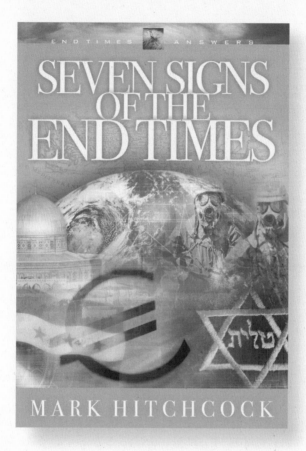

Americans are watching the news with expectant eyes, full of apprehension about what will happen next. Is it too early to worry that the times are winding down? Mark Hitchcock, a Dallas Theological Seminary graduate and recognized expert on end-times theology, distills the seven essential signs of the end as foretold in the Bible. In this fifth book of his authoritative series on biblical prophecy, Hitchcock cuts straight to the heart of an urgent topic, providing the information people need as they try to evaluate the state of their world.

ISBN 1-59052-129-3

"THE END IS NEAR!"

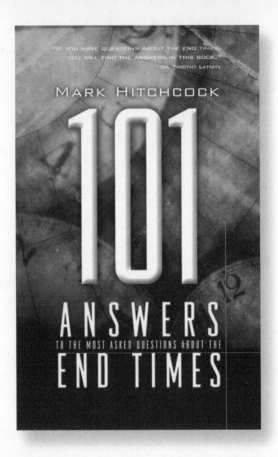

Or is it? The Antichrist is alive and well today! *Or is he?* The church is about to be raptured and will certainly escape the Tribulation...*right?* When it comes to the end times, there's so much confusion. Preachers with elaborate charts share their theories about Revelation and other prophetic books of the Bible. "Ah, Babylon stands for the United States," they say. But then other teachers share their theories: "No, Babylon stands for the Roman Catholic church, or the European Union, or the literal Babylon rebuilt in Iraq...." *Would somebody please shoot straight with me?* Finally, someone has. Gifted scholar and pastor, Mark Hitchcock, walks you gently through Bible prophecy in an engaging, user-friendly style. Hitchcock's careful examination of the topic will leave you feeling informed and balanced in your understanding of events to come...in our time?

ISBN 1-57673-952-X